SOUL CHATTER

A Guidebook to Gaining Fluency in the Language of Your Soul

Virginia Anne Corbett
Licensed Professional Counselor
Board Certified Coach

Renown
PUBLISHING
WRITE YOUR BOOK & REDEEM CULTURE

Renown Publishing
www.renownpublishing.com

Soul Chatter / Virginia Anne Corbett
ISBN-13: 978-1-960236-10-4

In celebration of my mother,
her reckless passion and her raucous laughter.

With unconditional love to:

my forever & always, John Charles;

the six most soul-filled humans I have ever met—
JAC, Chelsie & Timmy, Connyre & Dan;

and Augustus Charles, leading off the unfathomable joys
and promised sparkles soon to follow.

Love well. Be faithful. Keep the blessing!

Deus pascit corvos.

CONTENTS

The Genesis

I'll begin this book with its genesis story.

The greatest human gift I ever received was from my mother. The gift was a clean slate, the kind that comes only in the face of complete forgiveness.

Early one November morning, I crawled into her hospital bed and snuggled up to her, the way I always had when I was a child. "I love you, Mom," I whispered.

"I love you, too, Ginny. You know that's all that matters, don't you?" she assured me. A shiver rippled through my spine. My mother and I both shared the certainty that, when all was said and done, the love we shared really was the only thing that mattered. Years of frustration, fighting, and thoughtlessness melted away. We both *knew* the depth of our feelings. Authentic, unconditional love began its work of healing old wounds.

My mother had never been on time for anything in her life. She continued that tradition with her request to delay her funeral six months after her passing so it could take place on the Fourth of July. That dark ripple in time gave me a season to grieve and consider as I wrote her eulogy. Grief is an individual, unpredictable, and hazy journey. No two people grieve the same.

During that time, I was able to spend many hours thinking about the meaning of my mother's life and why she did the things she did. I wrestled with the complexities of our relationship and tried to make sense of some of her choices. In the process, I gained new and comforting insight. In my effort to make sense of my pain, I began writing.

And I kept writing. For ten years I wrote. My prose began as a tribute to the strong and courageous women I have known, which I entitled *Letters to the Women I Love.*

I also continued my career as a licensed professional counselor and led healing workshops. I was privileged to work with clients who were undergoing their own self-harmonization journeys. The healing patterns I observed and began researching became my self-harmonization model. I compiled personal exercises to effectively assist people as they moved through their pain.

It won't surprise you that my life and my passion overlapped and grew to create something beyond myself. This guidebook is the product of that passion. It is my Soul Chatter message, and my hope is that it will be helpful for fellow sojourners on their journey to becoming their best self.

I have learned a great deal as I have spent thousands of hours wrestling with the intricacies of emotional wellness. It is apparent to me that, although there is wholeness and restoration to be gained from the healing process, there first exists a bruised and painful wound to the soul. It is never a pleasant aspiration to face our fears and engage the emotions we've been stockpiling, for sorting out at a "more convenient" time. But the alternative is to live a life with less than our authentic effort. *Soul care* is beginning the quest to sort through those things holding us back from being our best self.

My own healing journey continues, and I have tried to be true to my own Soul Chatter. But at the end of the day, when the lights are dimmed and I find myself longing for an unmasked conversation with someone who knows my soul and relishes the humor in the moment, I come full circle to the same thought:

I miss you, Mom.

Me: Hey God.

God: Hello...

Me: I'm falling apart. Can you put me back together?

God: I would rather not.

Me: Why?

God: Because you aren't a puzzle.

Me: What about all of the pieces of my life that are falling down onto the ground?

God: Let them stay there for a while. They fell off for a reason. Take some time and decide if you need any of those pieces back.

Me: You don't understand! I'm breaking down!

God: No—you don't understand. You are breaking through. What you are feeling are growing pains. You are shedding the things and the people in your life that are holding you back. You aren't falling apart. You are falling into place. Relax. Take some deep breaths and allow those things you don't need any more to fall off of you. Quit holding onto the pieces that don't fit you anymore. Let them fall off. Let them go.

Me: Once I start doing that, what will be left of me?

God: Only the very best pieces of you.

Me: I'm scared of changing.

God: I keep telling you: YOU AREN'T CHANGING! YOU ARE BECOMING!

Me: Becoming who?

God: Becoming who I created you to be! A person of light and love and charity and hope and courage and joy and mercy and grace and compassion. I made you for more than the shallow pieces you have decided to adorn yourself with that you cling to with such greed and fear. Let those things fall off of you. I love you! Don't change! ... Become! Become! Become who I made you to be. I'm going to keep telling you this until you remember it.

Me: There goes another piece.

God: Yep. Let it be.

Me: So ... I'm not broken?

God: Of course not! —but you are breaking like the dawn. It's a new day. Become![1]

—John Roedel

INTRODUCTION

How to Use Your Soul Chatter Guide
A Brochure for Your Self-Harmonization Journey

Of this I am certain: fully harmonized people are fluent in the language of their soul.

One of my greatest joys has been witnessing the rebirth of a wounded soul, as the shattered pieces become whole with hope. The ever-present desire to piece together the broken shards of our lives creates the courage we need to press on in our journey of wholeness and wellbeing.

There is a wonderful Greek word that encapsulates complete healing: *sozo*.[2] This is the healing of our entire being—physically, mentally, and spiritually—all at one time. It is the state of complete salvation and ultimate peace.

We do not need an invitation to consider embarking on a sozo journey of deep healing and personal authenticity; all of us are already somewhere on this path. Knowing this, I encourage you to be intentional and to consider where you are on your voyage and what you desire from this life.

Your sozo journey will be unique; in fact, no two have ever been identical. If and how you intentionally conduct your trek—and when you move to the next step—is your decision, and yours alone, to make. The journey can be arduous, and there are times when we can all use and / or offer support to our fellow trekkers. We do this by encouraging each other's efforts and recognizing each other's gifts.

In truth, each of us has the ultimate freedom over our choices. The story of our own life is always ours to write.

The Sozo Journey to Soul Chatter Fluency
How It Begins: Forgetting Who We Are

For most of us, life begins as a carefree dance. As young children, we do exactly what we desire, unhampered by the opinions of others. If we want to play, we frolic. If we want to puddle splash, we jump in the mud. We are unabashedly ourselves as we skip through the meadow catching butterflies. But all too soon something changes.

Whether it's a singular, emotionally damaging event or a repeated chipping away, at some point we surrender and let the voices from the outside world become louder than the whispers of our own heart. To do this, we disengage with a fundamental part of ourselves. At that exact moment, we no longer recognize our Soul Chatter.

What, exactly, is Soul Chatter? By this I refer to the utterances deep within our soul. Fluency in Soul Chatter is achieved as we master the ability to connect and interpret the knowing of our being. It entails quieting the world and listening to our inner voice—or, in other words, being harmonized in who we are and committed to our purpose. Our fluency in Soul Chatter diminishes as we bend to satisfy the demands of the people around us.

Too early in childhood we begin to tally a lifelong list of our so-called flaws. If we could only fix this or change that, then maybe the people in our lives would be happy, and we would *finally have value*. Bit by bit, we become convinced that we are unacceptable and that we should suppress our core traits, which we have begun to see as unworthy. We begin to buy into the lie that our core self, our spirit, is unpresentable. We come to believe that our value is determined by the opinion of others. We conform and alter the traits that are the center of our being. The nips and tucks we make on our authentic self could be likened to personality surgery: a *person-ectomy*.

In time, we lose connection with who we really are and come to suspect that our inner being is unpresentable. Naturally, we bury it away from the world. That deceptive line of thought begins a lifelong journey of inauthenticity.

Other people's opinions become our measuring rod and hold the power to inflict emotional wounds. We become convinced of our flaws, and our worth becomes dependent on the connection, rejection, or approbation of others. We avoid opportunities to deeply and authentically connect with the people in our lives because we fear letting them see what is at the depths of our soul.

We feel lonely and unheard. We believe no one understands who we are and we must never let them know. We are no longer comfortable in our own skin. We stray from the path toward our authentic self. This is how we come to question our worth and lose sight of our purpose. This is the trap that leaves us deeply wounded, doubting our value and losing our voice.

The following manual is meant to guide you on your journey to an authentic life by sparking your being with practical methods to help you recognize patterns and break free of cycles. The seven steps that lead to self-harmonization are identified and broken into three phases: Soul Care, Soul Song, and Soul Soaring.

Phase I: Soul Care

You might consider *soul care* to be the care and feeding of your soul, and it begins with awareness. In our human condition we can neglect parts of our being and become hardened to the whispers of our soul. Although we are capable of living large, we distort memories and stomp down feelings. Emotions soon overflow and dwell in our dreams. At that point, the inner struggle between our dreams and our fears can manifest as self-sabotage, and we find ourselves on the battlefield of our war-torn mind.

None of us escapes unscathed. We all harbor an emotional wound in some stage of healing. It may be newly minted, or it may have become a calloused and familiar friend. At times, we all feel frustrated and held back by the world's web of opinions and judgment, while wrestling with the feeling that we are meant for more.

As you begin to pursue your healing journey, take heart—you are not alone. Tucked within your being is your Soul Chatter message and a passion to share it with the world. You get one time on earth to unveil the message that bubbles deep from within your being.

Phase II: Soul Song

A *soul song* can be a real song that wells up in our being or energy that culminates into a dance when our body feels authentically connected. This stage of Soul Chatter fluency is a time of ah-ha moments and powerful connection. We can overcome oppression and our past emotional pain as we experience contentment and realize our value and find our voice.

However, contentment is not complacency. We can take a deep breath, close our eyes, and imagine a life of being authentically connected with our soul. The persistent squawks and unwelcome interruptions of our unrelenting, opinionated world are stilled, and we retreat inward. At this moment our soul spontaneously breaks out in a song of profound joy, experiencing life as we were meant to live it.

Phase III: Soul Soaring

The freedom to be your authentic self and access the wisdom of your being is the best way to describe *soul soaring*. If the mental image of following your passion and living your purpose brings a smile to your face and quickens your heart, you already fly with the eagles.

The joy and pain we experience in this life—and how we choose to respond—is unique and varied. When we intentionally embark on our self-harmonization journey, there will be a moment when the pieces click together and point toward something greater. Our emotional wound will make sense as it becomes part of our story and vitalizes our being. Our courage and resolve will strengthen as the energy we previously used to struggle against our pain is, instead, used for creativity and loving others well.

The purpose of our struggle is realized in our *butterfly moment* of self-harmonization. The scars of our healed wound desire to give back and invigorate our passion.

In my work as a therapist, the reality of commonalities and patterns in the healing journey became inescapable. From years of observation, I developed and trademarked the Corbett Self-Harmonization Model™ to graphically illustrate each step of the Soul Chatter journey.

Modern lingo is fond of referring to becoming a better version of self as *leveling up,* but the best descriptor I have found for those determined people who choose to gut out their self-harmonization journey is that they achieve Soul Chatter fluency. They experience completeness and no longer feel the need to hide parts of themselves from the world. I encourage you to review each step before embarking on your heart-journey through this guidebook.

Corbett Model of Self-Harmonization

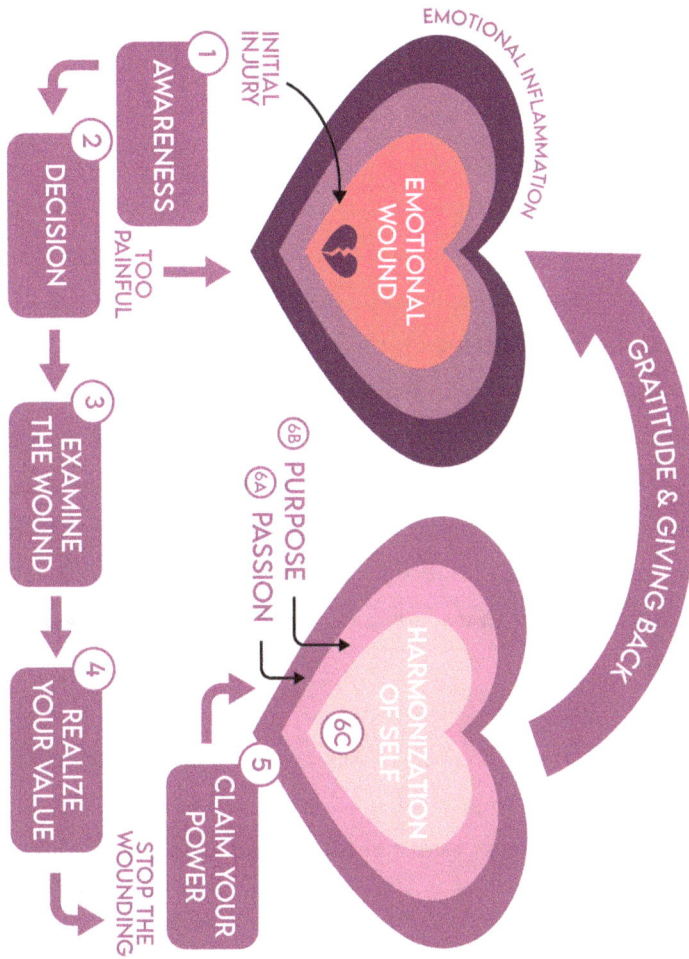

EMOTIONAL INFLAMMATION

INITIAL INJURY

1 AWARENESS

TOO PAINFUL

2 DECISION

3 EXAMINE THE WOUND

4 REALIZE YOUR VALUE

STOP THE WOUNDING

5 CLAIM YOUR POWER

EMOTIONAL WOUND

6B PURPOSE

6A PASSION

HARMONIZATION OF SELF

6C

GRATITUDE & GIVING BACK

An Overview of Steps 1–7

Corbett Model of Emotional Healing & Self-Harmonization™

Step 1: Awareness

Here you are.

You have arrived at the first step of your healing journey toward self-harmonization and becoming your best self. Just as you are beginning to relax and survey the grounds, one of your snarky *inner children* pipes up: "Am I on the journey, too? I don't remember getting a passport."

You may be hearing a lot from that one on this quest, but let's reassure him, "Yes, we are all on this journey, whether we consciously realize it or not." The first step of living your life on your terms is simply *awareness*.

Consciously and subconsciously, the power of the unfinished business of our past emotional injuries can paralyze us from becoming our best self. It demands our attention. It's an unfulfilled story that our psyche wants to control and play out as it attempts to finish the script of our life differently.

This pain may wrestle for power over how we choose to live our lives. We may let it dictate our perceptions and interfere with how we act and connect. Ultimately, we give our wound the power to undermine our sense of worth. Awareness can stop this downhill slide.

Step 2: The Decision

Once you gain awareness of your emotional wound and its power over your life, you will be faced with the decision to either examine the wound (Step 3) or return to a state of awareness (Step 1).

The decision to examine the wound can be life-changing, but many people get stuck on this step. Common obstacles in the path forward are external roadblocks (the people in your life) and internal roadblocks (self-sabotage). You may choose to return to a state of semi-awareness if you feel it's not the right time or if it's too painful to begin this journey (Step 2a). Whatever you choose, it's okay. Give yourself grace. You will know when you are ready.

The decision to let go of past patterns (Step 2b) and move to the next step on your personal journey to self-integration (or not) is one only *you* can make. You must make the intentional decision to progress to examining the wound (Step 3). Otherwise, it is inevitable that you will return to the familiar patterns of the past.

Step 3: Examine the Wound

Examining an emotional wound is much like treating a physical injury. The wound site is tender, and careful cleansing reveals unexpected gravel or debris. This is like encountering unforeseen emotional triggers.

Cleansing an emotional wound can be painful, but it's essential for an authentic journey. Remember, just as with a physical wound, cleansing and removing toxic debris will allow true healing to begin.

Step 4: Realization of Value

Understanding our value on a profound level changes everything. Not in a heady, egotistical way, but as worthy humans viewing ourselves as a vital part of something greater. This realization helps us internalize our place and purpose on this earth and puts our life and mission into perspective as it sparks an honest urgency.

We experience the freedom of realizing that our worth is not dependent on other people's opinions. We don't need anyone's permission to pursue our passions and live a life of purpose. Once we truly embody our worth, we will feel compelled to pursue our best self.

Step 5: Claim Your Power and Find Your Voice

Upon embracing our value, we can no longer allow abuse of our beings. Some of the boundaries we may have previously allowed others to violate or abuses we may have overlooked are no longer acceptable. The lies and false premises that exist in our relationships become apparent. We find our voice as we speak up for our needs and beliefs.

As we claim our power, pain is honestly addressed, and unhealthy relationship patterns are modified. In victory, we rewrite our pain-perspective, and we begin to view life through a new lens. The power of our aggressors is put in perspective and weakens as our personal strength is revitalized. At last, the inner child who has been protecting us from our pain has a voice.

Step 6: Harmonization of Self

Harmonization of self is a step with multiple stages, each assisting your reconnection with your inner being. You have given grace to your emotional wound and now see yourself as a victor, not a victim. You feel comfortable being your authentic, unabashed self and experience the full spectrum of appropriate emotions in the present moment.

In this step, you comprehend your Soul Chatter as you acknowledge the call of your heart and become serious about the importance of your passions. You experience inner contentment in your purpose.

Step 7: Gratitude and Giving Back

The final step of the self-integration journey is no longer about you. The energy spent and the clarity received through the process of leveling up and becoming fluent in your Soul Chatter produces an overwhelming sense of gratitude. You prosper from the wisdom gained in your journey and feel compelled to reach out and help other hurting people. This other-centered attitude adds purpose to your own journey and brings the healing process full circle.

Now, we will begin the first section of the book by exploring how to transform our life through soul care: awareness of our wound (Step 1) and making decisions about whether and when to examine that wound for healing (Step 2).

SECTION ONE: SOUL CARE
Self-Care That Transforms Lives

Section One Letter from Virginia

Dear Soul-journer,

Well done. As you read this, you are taking an intentional step on your best-self journey. This journey is unique, just as you are. Understand that the world needs what you have to offer, and you deserve to be energized with the exhilaration of a life well lived. But let's walk before we run and strengthen our wings before we fly. As we become aware of our Soul Chatter journey, it is essential that we internalize the importance of nurturing and connecting with our soul: Soul Care.

Soul Care begins with a brave awareness and an earnest desire to hold our place in the fabric of humanity. Great things are worth fighting for. Let's refuse to accept "someday" for an answer. Every Soul Chatter journey is unique, but there are common patterns. This guide is designed to help you recognize those patterns, affirm that you are on the right track, and (perhaps) muster the courage to go through the open door that calls your name.

The first step is to begin—and you just did.

Congratulations!

Virginia

Section One Preface

Soul Care is the first leg of our journey and Section 1 of your Soul Chatter Guide to becoming your best self. This section covers Steps 1 and 2 of the Corbett Model of Emotional Healing & Self-Harmonization™.

Step 1 is the *awareness* of our emotional wound. How do we get emotionally wounded in the first place? This world has a pattern of sending messages that we are *not enough*—not smart enough, not lovely enough, not wealthy enough, and (perhaps the most manipulative of all) not hurt enough. Feeling as though we are *not hurt* enough to identify our emotional wound and allow the awareness that leads to healing is the straitjacket of emotional healing.

Over the years, I have had clients who were excited to begin their Soul Chatter journey, only to hit pause as they contemplate the pain in the world. As they empathize with the more graphic, more recent, or longer struggles others have suffered, they feel guilt for their own healing. They hesitate and think, "Is it fair of me to complain? There are so many people with worse problems." This thought pattern becomes a lifestyle, and they find themselves stuck—too healthy to ask for help and too bruised to fly. Awareness changes this.

Step 2 is the *decision* to either (a) declare our emotional wound too painful to address until a better time or (b) explore it now. There is no wrong decision, and if we choose to wait, we will know when we are ready to honestly explore the condition of our emotional wound.

When we choose to explore our emotional wound (Step 2b), we can't help but recognize we have been holding the key to a life of passion and purpose. We begin our Soul Chatter journey as work on the pain that's been blocking our inner connection and shine a light on those dimly lit passages. We can be honest about our needs and reach beyond words to understand the utterances of our soul.

CHAPTER ONE

Step 1: Awareness

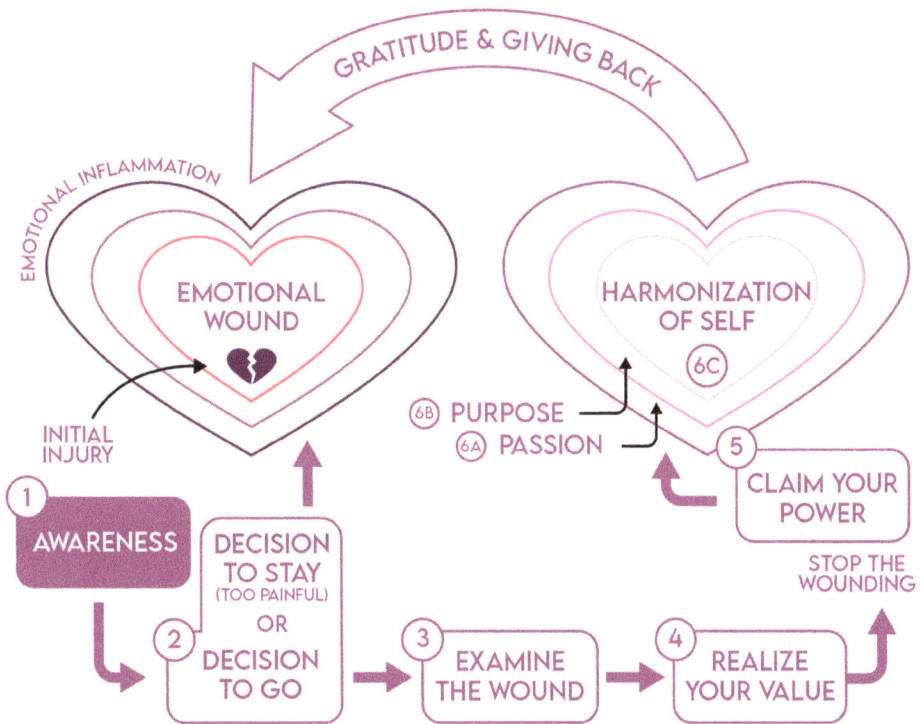

Corbett Model of Emotional Healing & Self-Integration™

> Life's a banquet and most poor bastards are starving to death.[3]
> **—Auntie Mame**

Deep breath. So, it begins.

Every epic adventure begins with a single, intentional act. The heroine musters what has been brewing in her soul and converts it into an action, an utterance, a defiant stand, or a single step.

Are you ready to live intentionally? Are you ready to embrace the life that calls you? Life is an arduous journey, but if you're willing to accept the challenge, living authentically will fire your passions and lead you to your purpose. This is Soul Chatter fluency, a state of authentic connection with your inner being while maintaining awareness of the dynamics of the external world.

Authentic living is the persistent quest to acknowledge your less-than-polished parts and those quirky desires that whisper from the depths of your being. It is a call rooted within your core; this is your Soul Chatter. You may choose to block it out by focusing on the business of life, or you can lean in and become aware of its beckoning.

Learning the language of your soul and trusting your intuitions may nudge you toward something that seems distant or outlandish. There are always risks. But what if that Soul Chatter has been drawing you toward the self-harmonization necessary for something greater? Perhaps your magnum opus? Choosing to ignore your Soul Chatter may be the biggest risk you ever take.

Step 1—Awareness

The first step to achieving emotional healing and self-harmonization is to simply be aware of our surroundings (both externally and internally). This is the act of living in the present moment. Living in the now requires both awareness and letting go. In order to embrace the life that is happening all around us, it is necessary to let go of distractions that cause us to detach.

We are invited to put down our screens, get out of our heads, and focus on life as it is unfolding in the moment. Intentional awareness allows an intimate present-moment connection as we experience the cooing of a dove or the gentle rain on a windowpane. This isn't just background noise, but an opportunity to witness the world that is unfolding in our midst. Connecting to what is authentic is present-moment awareness and an essential practice for soul care and living our best life.

Awareness is powerful.

Awareness is courageous.

Awareness changes everything.

Internal Awareness

In our chaotic culture, where kudos and cash flows are realized by focusing on our schedules and the check marks on our to-do lists, it can be extremely difficult to make time for inward focus. But success isn't rewarding if our mind is never hushed and anxiety sets our agenda. The antidote is to balance the outward demands with internal calm. Internal awareness means quieting our mind chatter to be aware of our Soul Chatter. It is the beginning of contentment.

Internal awareness seems like a simple practice, but it takes a great deal of determination. However, you will come to see that it is well worth your effort. There are many avenues to present-moment awareness, and some will feel more natural than others: meditation, prayer, yoga, woodworking, painting, baking, gardening (pick your expression). Find your Soul Chatter muse.

Intentional internal awareness is the practice of allowing our own voice to weigh in on what is important on our journey. Here we create a safe place as we shut out the world's judgment and opinions, as well as our own mind chatter. We can relax our body and just be. The resulting connection is a necessary step in our effort to become comfortable in our own skin—accepting all of who we are, right in this moment. This is *not* adoring and longing for the person we used to be or plotting and waiting for the person we could become. This is being honest about where we are, in this moment.

Self-acceptance is one of the most difficult tasks of being an emotionally balanced human. Our faults, our flaws, and our peccadillos are ever before us. But it will not be possible to authentically express unconditional love for anyone else until we first wholeheartedly accept the value of the soul within our being.

Emotional Toxins

As we probe inward, we will be increasingly conscious of our toxic thoughts and the emotional energy that resides in our core in the form of pain or emotional wounds. Strong emotions are energy that stimulate our minds and bodies. When those emotions are painful, they may exist as anxiety or trauma. It is common to have spent much of our lives doing an elaborate dance to avoid confronting our emotional wounds.

It is instinctive to disconnect from anything that is hurtful. We may live with a hailstorm of emotions, or we may have become emotionally numb. Both are ways to disconnect from our core self so we can avoid experiencing our true feelings. The problem with ignoring or avoiding our emotional hurt is that neither of these techniques will heal us. Even if we don't acknowledge the trauma, the pain won't go away.

Allowing ourselves to become aware of our truth and acknowledging the existence of toxic thoughts and energy is a courageous and vulnerable choice to make. There is a reason we have been packing away those feelings all this time. Once we acknowledge and face the pain, we can quit fearing these emotions.

When we numb or avoid emotional pain, we lose touch with a host of feelings—not just the ones we have been avoiding (such as fear and rejection) but also the ones we chase (like joy and contentment). We can't have it both ways. Either we can choose to have inner awareness and be in touch with our emotions, or we can pack them all away and build an emotional wall, brick by brick.

An unexpected win of getting in touch with those negative feelings you have been avoiding is the ability to reconnect with the emotional depth you have been craving. Be assured that there is a great deal of gratitude and love that has been locked away in your emotional vault as well.

An Awareness Story:
Embracing the Breeze

Erin had the most beautiful piercing green eyes. Though her eyes were bright, her face was sallow, and she looked ten years beyond her age. During our first therapy session, she described herself as sad and occasionally angry. Erin was a mother of two small children, and her husband's job demanded much of his time. Her own mother was an abyss of need and was a seasoned sniper heavily armed with guilt.

" 'Guilt: the gift that keeps on giving,' is our family motto," Erin joked, wincing, and then proceeded to hide her emerald eyes by staring at the floor.

When Erin first met with me, she reported that she had spent most of the past decade taking very good care of the people she loved. "Acts of service are my love language. Caring for people is what I naturally do. To please the people in my life, I multitask as a nurse, au pair, friend, chief cook, and bottle washer. Making my life work is like juggling an astronomical number of plates in the air for a very long time. My life has become a circus act, and I am the exhausted performer." The problem was that, lately, Erin's circus act had begun leaving a trail of broken glass, as each plate came crashing down one at a time.

Erin noted that she slept poorly and hate-ate lousy food, residing in a chaotic state of being "stressed out" most of her waking hours. And one more thing—she was smoking more weed than anyone knew. She was lonely, desperate, and felt completely out of options. "I have talked about my frustration ad nauseum to my husband and mom. I don't think they listen to me anymore—if they ever did. I wish they would understand how desperate and lost I really am."

Erin longed for deep, authentic connection. She felt worthless and questioned her value as a wife, mother, and daughter. As we dug deeper, she began to realize that she even questioned her value as a human.

Erin needed help untangling the knotted strings of her chaotic life. So, we began, thread by thread, gently sorting and making sense of the confusion. Like many women, Erin had taken top-drawer care of everyone in her life—except for herself.

You can only pour yourself out for so long before there is nothing left in your vessel. "I just want to be whole. I just want to be *me* again. I'm not even sure what I want or who I am anymore." She did not have the energy for even the most basic tasks, much less enough to put the pieces of her life back together.

The ironic thing about self-care is it can only be administered by your*self*. That day, Erin committed to embark on a journey of emotional healing and authentic living. In that moment, she chose to live a life that would respect her inner being. So, we began with an honest assessment of Erin's habits and dynamics, and we identified patterns that supported the lack of connection and inner chaos she was experiencing.

Erin perceived her greatest value as a nurturer and caretaker. Whenever *anyone* in her life needed *anything* done, they called on Erin. She had collected a number of five-star caretaker roles that required more time than she actually had. She made her boss very happy when she agreed to be the person to stay late on Fridays to close the office. She had volunteered as treasurer of the PTA at her children's elementary school for the past three years and was the designated ticket collector for her son's soccer league—because "no one else was willing to do *those jobs*."

Her time at home was completely overbooked with managing and supplying five people's schedules. Her mother had become dependent on Erin for daily visits and random errands, especially after the previous year's health crisis. Erin had been tremendously successful at bettering the lives of the people she loved, but she never had the life balance to put energy into her own needs. She was only just realizing this was connected to her utter depletion.

"I wake up every morning as a total stress bucket with my mind racing and already exhausted. I'm not the mother I used to be. I spend a lot of time yelling at my kids. My husband avoids me, and honestly, I don't blame him. I snap at random strangers—I dare you to cut in front of me in line at the bank. To be honest, I don't like the person I have become, and I don't know how to debark from this crazy train."

Over time, we discovered that the chaos in Erin's life served a purpose. It consumed her and helped her avoid the thoughts in her head, protecting her from being conscious of her own emotional pain and helping her disconnect from both the world and her authentic self.

She had revealed early in our sessions that under her kind and sweet veneer she was angry ("really pissed off") at the people in her life who had let her down, especially at her mother for emotionally checking out and not being there when she needed her most.

It would be several years before Erin was ready to discuss the summer her mother left her with her abusive uncle when she was a teenager. "How could she have done that?" she would eventually ask me. "When I look at my children, I just don't understand how she could have been so oblivious."

The distractions and chaos in Erin's life had become habitual, even familiarly comforting. Her tumultuous life screamed louder than her inner voice. Erin oriented herself firmly in the future by overscheduling and obsessing about what might happen next. This allowed her to disengage with her inner core and avoid addressing the needs of her heart.

After nearly a year of honest self-examination and consciously allowing inner chaos to submit to occasional calm, Erin realized something. Her pattern of making herself indispensable to her family, coworkers, and friends might be harmful to all of them, but most of all to her. It left Erin with little energy to take care of her own needs and stopped her family from learning to be independent.

"The gift I can give to the people I love is roots and wings—roots for them to know I love them and wings so they can learn to do some things themselves."

Erin's hard work and willingness allowed us to develop a personalized healing recipe of breathwork, meditation, and self-talk exercises to calm Erin's soul and quiet the negative mantras that continually played in her mind.

Eventually, Erin would become fluent in her Soul Chatter by intentionally connecting with her inner core and acknowledging the pain she had kept bottled inside of her for so many years. But the first step was awareness and experiencing the freedom that inner peace would provide.

Sozo Awareness Exercise:
Connective Breathwork and Conscious Contemplation

Location, Location, Location—Part 1
Finding Your Location on Your Journey to Self-Harmonization

<u>Intention</u>: This is a mindfulness exercise used to support an intentional exploration of where you are in your personal self-harmonization journey to Soul Chatter fluency.

<u>Materials</u>: A quiet place where you feel safe and comfortable and, if it's helpful, a copy of the graphic illustration of the Corbett Model of Emotional Healing & Self-Harmonization™.

Connective Conscious Breathwork

The following instructions are for Basic Soul Chatter Connective Breathwork and can be useful for most Sozo exercises. This breathwork is done with the intention of calming the outside chatter and connecting the inner centers of consciousness. During this breathing exercise, you will focus on the cleansing and connective energy of your breath while being conscious of energizing and connecting your inner being.

Action:

Start by taking four or five deep breaths, slowly inhaling through your nose and exhaling through your mouth.

Consciously, relax your body and focus your attention on your breath. Notice how soothing the oxygen is to your body.

Pause. Smile.

Continue with eight to ten more breaths. As you take them, intentionally use your mind to follow the path the oxygen takes as it travels through your body.

Imagine with each breath that you are breathing energy in.

Focus on the airflow as it cleanses, energizes, and connects your consciousness centers and the nervous system. The gut is sometimes referred to as the second brain. The gut / brain connection and a healthy gut microbiome are important for good emotional health. For the purpose of this exercise, we will think of them as the consciousness centers.

Imagine energizing each area as you oxygenate that perceived location. At this time, connect:

- your cognitive consciousness (head)
- your nervous system (spine)
- your gut conscious center (diaphragm)
- your heart, representing emotions (chest)
- your inner voice (voice box)

Slowly and intentionally breathe through your nose.

As the air travels through your head, pause and imagine being energized. Check in with your mind (your cognitive consciousness).

Maintain awareness as you mentally follow the airflow down the back of your spine. Imagine opening the billions of pathways in your nervous system as you energize your cells. Breathe energy as you focus and connect with your nervous system.

Put your hand on your belly as you fill it with detoxifying oxygen and energy. Imagine connecting with the wisdom of your gut consciousness. Fill your diaphragm with enough air to physically make your stomach rise. (Note: This may be uncomfortable at first, as few of us actually breathe deeply enough to oxygenate our body properly.)

Now, release the air and imagine it traveling up the front of your body past your chest. Imagine it energizing your heart consciousness. During this exercise, acknowledge your psyche and appreciate its elaborate ability to hold emotions and protect you from feelings you were not ready to process.

As the oxygen travels past your voice box, pause and energize your inner voice. Does it have anything to say? No pressure—you do not need to think about a specific message. Just acknowledge your inner voice as you energize it and create awareness.

Lastly, exhale all the oxygen out of your mouth. All of it. Imagine expelling emotional toxins with the carbon dioxide.

Fantastic work! You are taking the first steps of self-harmonization and Soul Chatter fluency.

Pause.

Rest.

Relax.

Breathe.

Sozo Exercise:
Mindfulness

Location, Location, Location—Part 2

Finding Your Location on Your Journey to Self-Harmonization

Intention: Part 2 of this exercise is the personal exploration of your healing journey. The intention is *not* to stir up the details of your emotional wound but to provide you a structure for acknowledging your journey and to empower you to consider emotional healing and passionate living.

Materials: A graphic illustration of the Corbett Model of Emotional Healing & Self-Harmonization™ and a quiet place where you feel safe and comfortable.

Action:

Connective Conscious Breathwork: Once you learn and understand connective breathwork, you are ready to move on to the contemplative stage of this exercise.

Take three to seven Connective Breaths.

When you're ready, study the Corbett Self-Harmonization Model™ and reflect on your personal healing journey. Look carefully at the steps and consider what resonates with you. This is not an all-or-nothing proposition. You may be in two places on the model at this time, or you may have some unfinished work at an earlier stage. This is simply an invitation to reflect and consider your journey as you make the choice to be intentional about living your best life.

Note: It's okay if these answers do not become readily apparent. You can begin to trust your gut-conscious center. You have already done the difficult work of just becoming aware (Step 1).

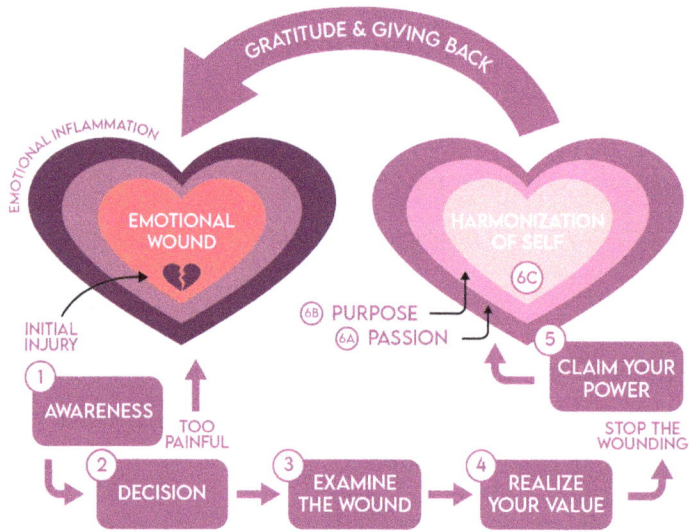

Corbett Model of Emotional Healing & Self-Harmonization™

Questions to consider as you study the steps to self-harmonization:

Ask your now-connected conscious, "Where am I on the self-harmonization journey?" Consider the first thing that comes to you and don't be afraid to do a brain dump.

_____

_____

_____

_____

_____

Take several conscious-connecting breaths and allow peaceful, empowering energy to guide you as you quiet your mind chatter. Visualize energizing your passion and using your personal gifts in a way that fills you. What would that look like?

_____

_____

_____

_____

_____

_____

Lean into the soothing experience of quieting the outer noise. Stretch your toes and breathe another connecting breath; expel all that oxygen. Experience listening to your Soul Chatter by focusing on your breath and quieting your thoughts. Be aware of the state of your being or the desires of your heart. Smile. You have begun your journey to _Soul Chatter_ fluency.

Journal
Feel free to add any additional thoughts here.

_____

_____

_____

_____

_____

_____

_____

_____

_____

_____

_____

Mindful External Awareness

All of us can benefit from external awareness. Understanding the atmosphere is imperative for any good pilot to take flight. Without external awareness and clear boundaries, the demands of the outside world will inevitably consume our personal energy and deplete our resources, leaving little reserve for us to experience contentment or sustain an internal calm.

The quest to maintain a balanced, healthy state of being requires us to assert solid emotional boundaries and to discern where our being stops and the outside world begins. Only then can we make an informed choice as to what in this life is worth investing our personal energy in.

One awareness technique that many people find effective is Reporter Mode. (You can find detailed instructions for this method in the Sozo Awareness Exercise at the end of this chapter.) Reporter Mode is a technique for making a safe space from which to observe relational energy dynamics as they play out in our environment without getting pulled into outside chaos.

Awareness of Our Surroundings

As we develop our external awareness, we can consciously examine the connections that influence our life and our decisions. Consider our circles of influence, starting at the center and moving outward: (1) the immediate environment, including intimate relationships; (2) community, including casual relationships; and (3) global culture and its influence on our worldview.

ENERGY DIAGRAM

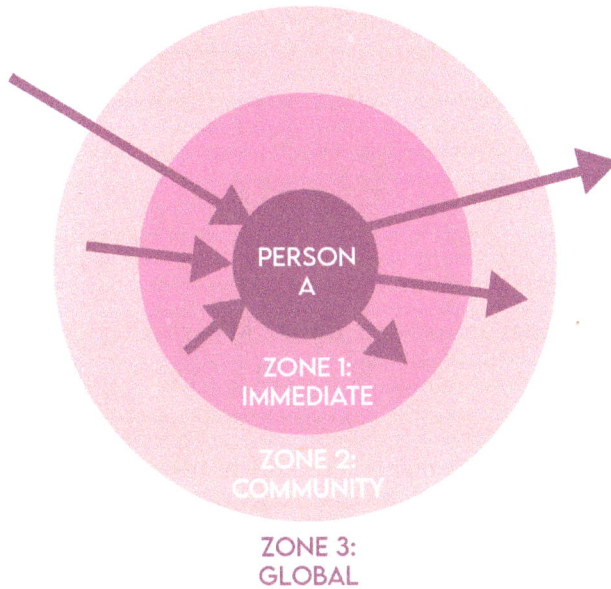

PERSON A

ZONE 1:
IMMEDIATE

ZONE 2:
COMMUNITY

ZONE 3:
GLOBAL

Awareness of Zone 1
Immediate Environment, Including Intimate Relationships

The closest of the concentric circles in our external connections is our direct environment and tight-knit relationships: our families, partners, and close friends. This is where we *likely* have the greatest immediate connection, and it is also where toxic or negative energy and unhealthy relationship patterns have a direct effect on our day-to-day living.

A first step as we strive for healthy connections within our immediate environment is *awareness* (Step 1). Using the Reporter Mode technique, we simply observe the personal energy in our relational dynamics (both productive and toxic), noticing the origin of the energy, the route it takes, and the type of energy each player in our life brings into our environment.

The personal nature of our Zone 1 relationships makes it challenging to step back and remain objective. We are tempted to react or assert control. But we are data-gathering, and it is important that while in awareness mode we commit to observation and resist the urge to engage. Remember, we are making long-term changes for both ourselves and the people we love. With our efforts, we can identify and modify generational patterns (both healthy and toxic) that have been handed down to us.

In the early stages of therapy, clients often devote a large portion of their time and energy to unraveling the mysteries of their intimate relationships. Whether it be a spouse, a family member, or a close friend, we perplex each other. "Why would they do that?" "Did they really say that? What did they mean by that anyway?" We hold on to the illusion we can control other people's actions. In the end, the only power we have is the choices *we* make in any given situation.

I once heard a man talking about the good boundaries he kept in his home. He taught his children these same boundaries by taking them to the window and explaining to them that the things occurring in the world were outside their control and they could not fix them. Instead, they could control what went on in their immediate environment, and their family would commit to being a place where love was spoken. That family made the choice to maintain healthy relationships and cultivate positivity within the walls of their home. Intentional healthy boundaries and mindful awareness of their environment was the key to their commitment and the roots of a contented life.

Note: If your intimate relationships leave you baffled, never fear. There is an entire chapter of this manual ("It's All Relatives") that is devoted to shining light on relationship dynamics.

Awareness of Zone 2
Community Relationships

As we step further out in our circles of external awareness, the next space where personal energy is exchanged is Zone 2. The relationships on this level tend to be more transitory than those in our immediate environment, but they are often impactful, as the frequency and significance of these connections make them important.

In this modern world, it is impossible to shelter in the sanctuary of our homes without the unrelenting messages (both positive and toxic) of our extended relationships ricocheting into our personal lives and affecting our emotional wellness. The disparate power dynamics of institutions and work environments are inherently riddled with exploitation. Power games, such as bullying and sexual and emotional abuse, are rampant and too often institutionally accepted.

Like our awareness of the energy dynamics of Zone 1 (our immediate relationships), the first step to setting boundaries for Zone 2 (our work and communities) is to calmly observe dynamics on all levels, while remaining wary of the toxic energy influence of gossip, hype, and peer pressure.

Intentionally setting professional boundaries and keeping these relationships in perspective is imperative in our effort to prevent desensitization. Many institutions and community groups that we must interact with can skillfully pull us into their chaos. But their toxic energy is not our toxic energy and does not need to become a part of our story.

To be clear, there is nothing inherently negative about being part of a community group. Healthy groups can be positive and powerful and can change our world. Our involvement in them may even be part of our purpose. But without a clear external awareness of the dynamics and energy exchange of our communities, the pendulum can swing very quickly. When work-life balance suffers, it weighs on our emotional health and affects all of our relationships.

Awareness of Zone 3
Global and Cultural Relationships

The connection we have with the global culture and our awareness of its dynamics waxes and wanes over the course of our lives. To be certain, social media and the twenty-four-hour news cycle has spotlighted our connection to global events. Yet, most of the time, the culture at large seems removed from our day-to-day reality, and its personal impact is minimal. But there are times when awareness of the world comes crashing into our living rooms, and its influence on our lives is undeniable.

Every generation shares in, and is united by, global tragedies and victories. Events on this scale alter both our lives and the lives of the people we share them with. Depending on your age, you may remember exactly what you were doing on September 11, 2001, as the world was forever altered by those tragic events. Or, if you were alive in 1986, you will likely share in the collective memory of the *Challenger* space shuttle exploding on live television. You may be a bit older and remember the victories of sending a human to the moon or the fall of the Berlin Wall. Our global-level connections—the victories and the tragedies—are shared events that unite us.

In the spring of 2020, a series of unprecedented events changed the course of a generation. As the new decade began, a pandemic erupted. In an effort to "flatten the curve" and save thousands of lives, most of the world went into a lockdown. Many people suffered, losing their loved ones, their jobs, and their businesses. They made personal and painful sacrifices in order to do their part.

As they pared down their schedules and checked out of their once chaotic lives to quarantine, they often found themselves experiencing an unfamiliar external calm. In this unexpected place of quiet, there was time for reflection.

In a very real sense, this forced calm produced a global awareness that had not been experienced in decades. In just a few months, sights and sounds were reported as more vivid. Long-term residents of New York City noted the sounds of bird songs they had never heard before. On a global level, the world shared an awareness of something beyond its usual distractions.

An unexpected outcome of the pandemic lifestyle for many people was a new awareness. Their retooled schedules forced them to reconsider the state of their relationships and the life balance that their pre-pandemic busyness had allowed them to avoid. Many mental health providers and addiction professionals noted that they were meeting with a new (often more motivated) population of clients who had never had counseling before and were finally ready to work on their emotional wellness.

There is a silver lining to even the darkest of clouds. For each of us, awareness of our global external connections shapes us in profound ways at unexpected times. Being a contributing member of society without taking on the collective toxic energy of the world is imperative to living an emotionally balanced life.

Using Awareness to Set Boundaries

Yes, I Own This Circus. But Is It My Responsibility to Calm the Escaped Monkeys?

Once we become aware of each zone's relationship dynamics and the personal energy exchanges that occur in our lives, the next step is to decide what we would like to do with that information. This is our story, and we might choose to change nothing at all. How we let our interactions affect us are based on the boundaries we set (or don't set). Our actions are our choice, but keep in mind—*we cannot change another person.*

Intentionally setting healthy boundaries in our lives (within each zone of influence) can be perplexing, but it sets a foundation for living a life of integrity. We can be responsible for only our side of the relationship equation. A helpful, time-tested method for sorting out boundaries and helping us recognize what is within our control has been used by addiction groups for decades. It releases the burden of responsibilities that are not ours, enabling us to make it through a dark night. We know it as the Serenity Prayer:[4]

> God, grant me the serenity to accept the things I cannot change, courage to change the things I can, and the wisdom to know the difference.

Sozo Awareness Exercise:
Reporter Mode

The Art of Observation

Intentional Awareness on Your Journey to Self-Harmonization

This exercise is designed to help sharpen your awareness of the dynamics that exist in your relationships. The purpose of this awareness exercise is to provide space so you might be able to observe what is happening around you without getting caught up in the immediate moment and being pulled away from a place of neutrality.

<u>Materials</u>: A thin slice of real life and extreme patience.

<u>Summary</u>: Reporter Mode is a technique for understanding the impact of relationship patterns. Instead of becoming engrossed in a situation, simply observe and note what is happening. This is an exercise that will become more natural as you practice this technique. It may be helpful to record your observations in a journal.

<u>To begin</u>: Consciously choose to record what is going on in the relationship dynamics as they are happening. It might be helpful to pretend that you are an old-fashioned Dick Tracy–type reporter writing a synopsis of the event.

_____

_____

_____

_____

_____

Imagine you are in the corner of the room and spend some time observing. Although you may have to react, try not to engage. Be conscious of the dynamics, not the content of what is happening. For example, you might note, *Frank was leaning in and looking intimidating as he talked about how broken he was. Emma looked nervous and tried to avoid eye contact with him. Both of them kept glancing at me as if they wanted me to intervene and make everything better.*

Those are the type of notes and observations that are made from Reporter Mode. Don't try to fix or judge anything; just notice patterns. Remember, words are 35 percent of communication[5]—there's so much in the message (inflection, body language, tone, and delivery) that we often miss when we get too entangled in the emotions of an interaction.

Mindful Awareness
Creating a Safe Space for Inward Focus

As we hone our greater external awareness of energy dynamics and opt to create and practice healthy boundaries, we will experience renewed personal energy and emotional reserves. We may now choose to change our focus from outward to inward.

This is a normal process, and to varying degrees we have been doing this all our life. But there are times when it may be helpful to create a safe area and allow time and space to intentionally focus on internal connection. With internal awareness, our core connection (Soul Chatter fluency) sharpens.

Heightened internal awareness overrides and quiets our mind chatter and allows us to be conscious of personal connections, as we grow more aware of energy exchanges and relationship patterns. Practicing this art increases our capacity for present-moment living and spotlights the contentment that derives from accepting the ebb and flow of existence.

Onward

Being intentional in our relationships and mindful of how we are affected by those connections is awareness (Step 1). You have taken the first step on your self-harmonization journey to Soul Chatter fluency. Noticing connection patterns will change the trajectory of your course. You got this!

It isn't the fast-paced, intrusive outside world that knocks us off our path; it is our own inner disconnection. This lack of awareness allows toxic chaos to deplete our resources and gives voice to those fear-thoughts that convince us we are not strong, we are not brave, and we do not have choices.

Self-harmonization and living your best life is a passionate, determined pursuit in which you claim your right to authentically live your life on your terms: creating, contributing, and loving well. The story of your life is yours to write. Consider this your Land of Oz, and *you* wear the magic red slippers. In the wise words of Glinda, the Good Witch of the South, "You have always had the power, my dear. You just had to learn it for yourself."[6]

Chapter One Notes

CHAPTER TWO

Step 2a: The Decision to Stay
Addressing Internal Setbacks on Your Self-Integration Journey

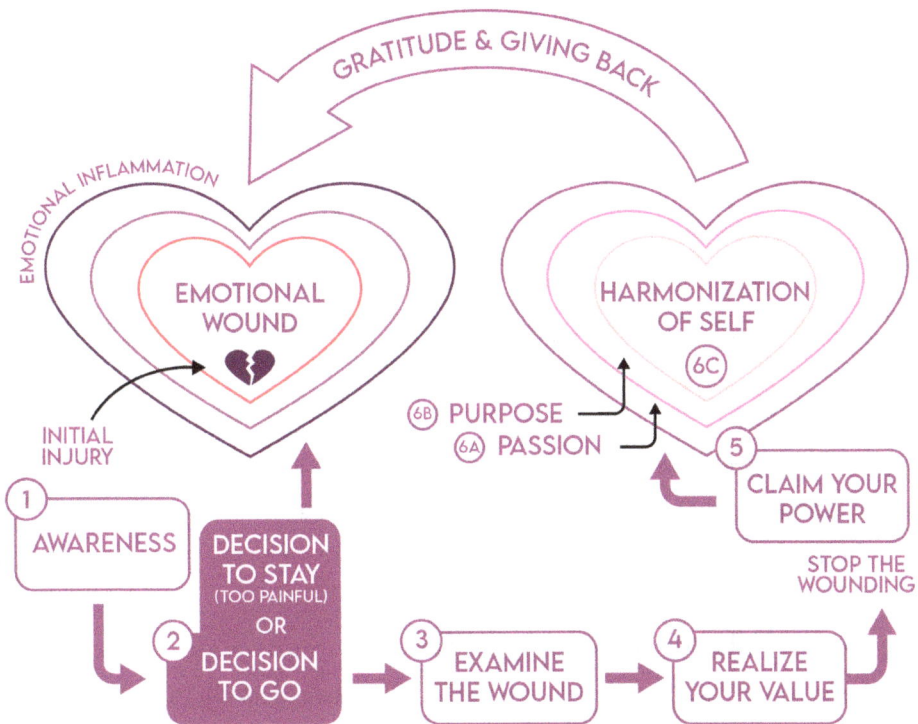

Corbett Model of Emotional Healing & Self-Integration™

Imagine yourself living in a space that contains only things that
spark joy. Isn't this the lifestyle you dream of?[7]
—Marie Kondo

Each of us has a guarded place in our being where dreams and passions reside. Our emotional wound does a valiant job of blocking entry to that sacred spot by being tender to the touch, chiding us about our aspirations, and using fear to remind us that we really don't want to risk access to anyone—not even ourselves.

Over time, our protected inner sanctum functions very much like that spare room in our homes where we ditch all our miscellaneous junk before company comes over. Clutter and trappings pile up to the point of embarrassment, so we close the door, bolt it shut, and pretend our lifelong accumulation of stuff doesn't exist. Out of sight, out of mind—except it isn't. Our emotional baggage weighs heavy on our minds, and the energy we spend cloaking it becomes exhausted.

Marie Kondo is a renowned organizer who has developed a unique method to help people declutter their spaces and enjoy their possessions by letting go of what they no longer need. Her approach involves holding and examining each item of clutter and keeping it if it "sparks joy" or gratefully releasing it if it does not.

Emotional clutter is similar. We might choose to hold on to emotional baggage (i.e., guilt, shame, perceived obligations, and worthlessness) that no longer serves a purpose and hinders us from living a life of passion, purpose, and contentment. On this journey, we will find it immensely helpful to honestly examine the fears that permit us to hold on to patterns and perceptions that may be blocking us from living the life we desire.

We may choose to hold on to the emotions that protect our wound, or we may decide to release them. In either case, facing our fears is a brave thing to do. With awareness (Step 1), the decision (Step 2) is inevitable, and we must decide, "Do we want to retreat and return to life as we know it, or are we ready to address our emotional wounds?"

We cannot authentically proceed on our self-harmonization journey until we make a conscious decision to enter that emotionally overflowing inner room that we have been desperate to avoid. It will be necessary to let go of our clutter in order to discover the reality of what has been obscured.

This chapter takes an honest look at the decision *not* to examine our wound at this time, to put off considering all the things holding us back until a better time (Step 2a). In the next chapter, we'll focus on the decision to face our fears, move forward with intentionality, and examine our emotional wound (Step 2b). There is no right or wrong decision; your choices are yours to make. At this time in life, you may decide to put your energy into day-to-day living.

It is important to note, however, that wound examination is necessary to thrive on the journey to self-harmonization. Although it is possible to skip ahead and tackle your passion and purpose (Step 6) without addressing your emotional wound (Step 3), there will be times of incompleteness. Soul Chatter fluency is a process of discovery. Allow time to be gentle with yourself; you will know when you are ready.

An Awareness Story: Self-Sabotage 101
Confessions of an Energy Vampire

What was inescapable about Vera was the exhaustion I felt every time I met with her. She was a kindhearted woman in her early sixties with a six-string Texas twang. She had a stocky build and shaggy ash-brown hair.

When Vera walked into the counseling room, she would make a beeline for the couch and begin her unique melting process—within ten to fifteen minutes, she would slide from a sitting position to fully lying down. During her digressions, I found myself feeling drained and tired. In time, it became apparent that Vera was an energy vampire.

A counseling session provides a mini slice of what's going on in the life of the client, a petri dish of their real-world dynamics. This makes it possible to observe relationship interactions and energy exchanges. Stress, anxiety, and depression are easy to identify. During the therapeutic relationship, a counselor may match the client's energy. In this setting, I instinctively matched Vera's lack of energy and became exhausted myself.

It took several months for Vera to recount her bad-luck story of near-successes and oppressive relationships. For the past decade, she had found herself at the mercy of her friends' sofas to keep her from being homeless. She had already been cut off from most of the relationships with her own family members.

The first treatment plan that Vera and I developed had a fairly low bar for success and had as its main goal a plan to work toward her being able to sustain herself. There are times in a person's life when not falling deeper into a hole is progress. We spent the six months of sessions working to keep Vera from regressing.

One spring day, Vera came through the door with a slight skip in her step. "I want to show you something I found last weekend." She handed me a crumpled, full-color pamphlet for a motivational conference. On the cover was a vivacious-looking blonde woman inviting people to attend. "This looks fun Vera, but this conference is over; it happened years ago."

"I didn't bring this in for me to go to the conference. I brought this to show you what I did twenty-five years ago," she explained. I blinked my eyes and took another good look at the pamphlet. *Was that actually her?* Wow. It was.

Vera had mentioned that she had done some public speaking, but this was a national conference and a big deal. I wondered, *What had happened for Vera to go from a dynamic, productive human to just living in survival mode?* She seemed compelled to answer that very question without my having to ask.

"I was a go-getter as a young woman, and a few times I had it all at my fingertips. But I never thought I deserved to have the finer things in life. I have never felt worthy. Every time my life was coming together, it felt wrong. I guess I wasn't built for the good stuff." I sighed, and we both shed a tear over such a sad revelation.

Vera had left a huge amount of living on the banquet table of life, and she knew it. I am a firm believer that it is never too late to regain the "years the locusts have eaten" (Joel 2:25 NIV), but some things in Vera's life were simply gone.

I would love to tell you that there was a happy ending to Vera's story, that she pulled it together and tapped into the energy and successes of her life. But that was not a choice I ever saw her make. Over the next few years that we worked together, she had some moments when her life was not falling apart and she felt hopeful, but never to the degree she was capable of.

Vera did not understand her value and did not believe she was worth fighting for. Her deeply ingrained patterns of self-sabotage were ones she chose to continue.

I share Vera's story not to dash your hopes but to give you perspective.

Every one of us is worth fighting for and is here for a purpose. You can claim this truth as yours and lean into the task at hand, or you can choose to let your one precious life flitter where it may. That choice is certainly yours to make. However, your Soul Chatter has a unique story to tell, and you are the only person who is fully qualified to author your adventure.

It's never too late to choose joy. The rest of your life starts with your next decision. When that tiny bit of verve sparks, fan the flame. Claim your worth and fight for the Soul Chatter aspiration necessary to fire your passion and live out your purpose. This is your journey to self-harmonization, and the specific details are yours to write. Recognizing your worth is the first step. I know you must claim this for yourself, but I assure you that you are worth it.

Are You a Self-Saboteur?

Most self-sabotage stems from a lack of faith in our ability to become our best self, from the internal disconnection that rejects the wisdom of our Soul Chatter. If you suspect you are a person who undermines your own success, torpedoes prospects for positive relationships, or undercuts opportunities when they present themselves, you may have a pattern of self-sabotage.

This can be even more jarring as we begin to realize that we may be continuing the cycle of abuse on our own person that someone else had started. Allowing ourselves the objectivity to honestly evaluate the fears that have contributed to our identity framework can be the pivot point for living our best life.

Cognitive Behavioral Therapy (CBT) is a method of identifying and examining flawed or outdated thought patterns and replacing them with true and productive thoughts.[8] Those negative life frameworks often contribute to destructive decisions and block us from living our best life.

You can choose this day to embark on a self-harmonization journey that rejects the fears and lies that keep you stuck. You can free yourself of *stinking thinking* and determine to embrace the opportunities and possibilities for thriving. Be expectant. Write your next chapter as you claim your passion, energize your resources, and live abundantly.

Sozo Decision Exercise:
Self-Sabotage

A Quiz
Understanding Your Sabotage Framework

Identifying fear-thoughts proves useful for understanding why we continue with behaviors we want to stop. Our psyche manipulates our behaviors by playing on our core fears with distorted frameworks and false narratives. Identifying and facing them down is liberating. You will recognize that the reality of the fear is often not nearly as ominous as it seemed in your mind.

The following test will help you identify which fear-thought area may be your Achilles' heel. For each prompt, circle the answer option that most resonates with you.

I am likely to quit my job because:

1. My boss promoted me into a new demanding position, but that job will limit my chances at something else.

2. Most of the coworkers I enjoy have already quit for other jobs.

3. The office doesn't seem very friendly. I just don't gel with that crowd.

4. I don't know if I have the skills to meet the demands of this job.

My last argument with a significant other stemmed from:

1. They wanted to be exclusive, and I am not ready for that.

2. I was sick of never having input when it came to big decisions.

3. My feelings were hurt because I never felt appreciated.

4. I will never be as good as their ex.

My financial woes are most likely caused by:

1. There was a huge sale on gear, and I needed some for my next adventure.

2. My friend talked me into a bad investment.

3. I end up buying lots of gifts and paying for other people's bills.

4. I am not very good at financial management.

I would most like to be thought of as:

1. Daring.

2. Bold.

3. Loved.

4. Valuable.

The most accurate motto for my life is:

1. The world is my oyster.

2. Last man standing.

3. The life of the party.

4. Can't live without me.

In this exercise, we examined four types of fear-thoughts. Each answer option corresponds to the following types:

1. Possibility fears.

2. Power fears.

3. Relationship fears.

4. Worth fears.

If you circled three or more of the same number, review the corresponding fear category detailed in the following pages as you identify and understand your root fears.

Understanding Fear-Thoughts

Moving forward in our self-harmonization journey requires shining a light on our fears and being honest with ourselves about the role they play in our lives. In order to identify false narratives, it is helpful to take an honest inventory. Examining our root fears—where they originated and their pattern in our interactions—is the first stage to replacing them with more productive thoughts.

Types of Fear-Thoughts

Fear frameworks are made up of several root fears. They can overlap and intermingle. Taking the simplified approach of examining each one on its own merit is a comfortable place to start. Most fear frameworks break into four overarching categories: Possibility Fears, Power Fears, Relationship Fears, and (the grandmother of them all) Worth Fears.

Note: Pay special attention to any fear that you may have identified as a hinderance from the Sozo self-sabotage quiz.

Possibility Fears

These fears often surface as you set out to do something audacious or are presented with an opportunity. They include, but are not limited to, fear of success, fear of failure, fear of decisions, and an addiction to possibilities.

Fear of Success: Avoiding success at any cost. The demands and obligations could be catastrophic. The possibility of changes to life and relationships are not worth the risk.

Fear of Failure: Avoiding challenging things. The risk of failure trumps the reward of success.

Fear of Decisions: Making a decision could eliminate many exciting prospects. The possibility of a negative outcome stops us from making a decision at all.

Possibility Junkie: Living in this saturated state is exhilarating and adrenaline producing. Possibility junkies get high on the idea of what *might be* and actively resist taking action.

Power Fears

Power. The very word causes a reaction in most people and often produces a myriad of forehead-rubbings and sighs. Power fears involve the connection and transfer of personal energy: who gets it, who keeps it, and who steals it.

The framework of most power fears is based on the concept of a nonrenewable power dyad, in which personal power is viewed as a limited resource. If you want more personal power, you must take it from someone else. (Note: This is not true and is a limited way to approach life. While there are obvious situations in which we can draw this conclusion, Soul Chatter fluency energizes personal power, essentially making it renewable.)

We can rework our power framework by realizing that engaging in our passions and purpose is energizing and that supporting the people in our lives by engaging in theirs is uplifting as well. This renewed, constructive power framework is supported by many positive philosophies, such as: win/win (when a transaction is positive for all engaged parties), golden bridges (when you build a positive path out of a difficult situation), and personal energy expulsion that renews energy (when engaging in some activities is energizing instead of draining).

Fear of Losing Control: Avoiding any situation where absolute control is not perceived as attainable. The possibility of losing control in a situation may cause self-sabotage. We may pull back from relationships, and there may be an associated anger or resentment.

Fear of Taking Control: Avoiding any potential for responsibility. Any hint of failure confirms the ultimate fear of being incapable or incompetent.

Power Junkie: Like most pleasure-inducing experiences, it is possible to be addicted to power. If you suspect this addiction is alluring to you, ask yourself if the perks of power—status, wealth, prestige, titles—have too great an influence on your thoughts and your motivations.

Relationship Fears

Authentically connecting with another human requires risk and vulnerability. All of us have been wounded in relationships. The choice to make ourselves vulnerable to that kind of pain again is a terrifying thought.

Relationship fears are a response of protection against further emotional pain.

Unfortunately, that pattern prohibits us from reaching the depths of sharing that is necessary to form future healthy relationships.

Fear of Rejection: Avoiding relationship connection will eliminate the possibility of future rejection, but also the chance for a relationship with depth.

Fear of Abandonment: Hyperfocus on the possibility that a close relationship will end in abandonment. Often stems from a traumatic experience or a perceived traumatic experience in which the person was significantly disappointed by a primary person in his or her life.

Fear of Intimacy: Avoidance of intimacy both physically and emotionally, most often from deep-rooted past abuse or abandonment.

Worth Fears

The fear that we are not good enough is the most disconnecting fear a person can have. It undercuts all joy and contentment. Once this fear has taken root, it is very difficult to combat. In all truth, I believe most of us wrestle with it in one form or fashion. This fear stems from the deep-rooted belief that "I am not good enough" or "I do not deserve to have the finer things in life." All other fears are to some degree entangled with this fear.

Fear of Mediocrity / Inadequacy: The tension between your desire to "be more" and the stress of doubting your ability.

Being Someone You Are Not to Make Other People Happy: Manicuring your behavior to fit the desires of another person and fearing that your thoughts or your dreams need to be validated by others. The danger is that at some point your authentic self will be lost in the image of who you portray.

How to Sabotage Self-Sabotage

Sabotaging self-sabotage is a battle for our lives—our best lives. We were made to do great things. But the hazy mist of fear obscures our views and blocks us from authentic living. Don't accept anything less than the life you deserve.

The next step on the journey to self-harmonization is to choose to reject untrue fear-thoughts and to connect to your Soul Chatter wisdom. Take a deep, calming breath, as this process may take you out of your comfort zone. It will also energize your passion and open the door to dare-to-dream possibilities.

As you push forward, expect resistance. With this in mind, it is helpful to create a toolbox with emotionally supportive methods that counter sabotaging behaviors. Here are a few helpful *sabo-tools* to use when you notice destructive patterns creeping into your actions.

Sabo-Tool #1: Know Yourself; Know Your Opponent

Arguably, one of the greatest battle strategists of all time was Sun Tzu, a Chinese military commander who lived in the fifth century BC. His battle strategy guide was made into a book. *The Art of War* has stood the test of time and, to this day, is used by military academies, business colleges, and athletes for insight into how to win battles. A primary tenet of Sun Tzu's battle strategy was to know yourself and to know your opponent.

Defeating self-sabotage is one of the most difficult battles we humans fight. Understanding both our own motives and the nuance of sabotage is important for personal victory.

> If you know the enemy and know yourself, you need not fear the result of a hundred battles. If you know yourself but not the enemy, for every victory gained you will also suffer a defeat. If you know neither the enemy nor yourself, you will succumb in every battle.[9]
>
> **—Sun Tzu**

Know Yourself

Soul Chatter fluency is the exploration of, and connection to, our inner parts. This is our avenue to self-knowing. Becoming comfortable in our own skin is necessary for contentment.

During the self-exploration process, we unpack the conflicting motives and methods within our being. I will refer to these central parts of our being as *inner children*. Understanding and practicing self-grace toward our inner children is a wonderful way to engage in soul care. And it can produce surprising results. With self-awareness, we gain understanding of the complexities of our own internal struggles.

Know Your Opponent

The primary strategy for defeating self-sabotage is to acknowledge its existence and become familiar with its deception. It is essential that we understand the pattern and source of a fear's roots. The irony of self-sabotage is that a part of ourselves is blocking our own progress. This may be one of our inner children asserting their agenda, often with what seems like good intentions.

Sabo-Tool # 2: Identify Patterns of Sabotage

With repetition, self-sabotage becomes a pattern. To identify the patterns that may thread through your life, it may be helpful to get a whiteboard, or pen and paper, and to physically list all the sabotage events you can remember. Consider the repeated behaviors that have kept you from taking your victory lap.

Root fears and generational patterns are often subconscious and automatic. The patterns and accompanying thought processes have made a well-carved trail and do not require conscious thoughts. Identifying these patterns enables us to make changes.

An example of a thought pattern is, "I seem to pick a fight with my partner before we visit his relatives. I think my fear is that his parents don't really like me, and I don't want to be rejected by them."

Recognizing and identifying the root fears behind sabotage gives you the option to make a different decision next time the situation arises. Or you can remain stuck in that thought pattern. Either way, it is a conscious determination, and you control the direction of your choice.

Now that you understand why you fight with your partner before you visit his relatives, you can choose to:

a) Tell him calmly that you don't want to go.

b) Reevaluate your relationship with his family.

c) Continue to have a disagreement before family events.

d) Brainstorm another option.

Sabo-Tool # 3: Reframe Your Sabotage Response

The Reframe is the action sabo-tool, and it has the power to change our lives. Self-sabotage is exhausting. Circular thinking and internal quarreling require a great deal of energy. We don't have to be stuck in that trap though.

As we envision and pursue audacious goals, it is natural for fear-thoughts to swing into action in an effort to restrain and safeguard us from being too vulnerable. The concept of actually living our big dreams can shake up our zen and draw us out of our comfort zone.

What if we believed we might really pursue a relationship with our soulmate? What if we dared to fuel our passion with the ideal career we have been longing for? What if we were the heroes in our own stories? These ideas are bold and, frankly, overwhelming. The journey to our dreams takes us away from the safety of our bubble, and if we commit to action, we will leave some familiar comforts behind.

Note: It is important to consider that some of the things we fiercely hold on to will not continue to be ours, even if we choose to stay in our comfort zone. Change is inevitable.

The Journey to Self-Harmonization Continues...

In the next chapter we will explore the decision to examine the wound (Step 2b). If you are ready to examine your emotional wound, you will feel compelled to do so. But if your choice is to examine your wound later, know that you have come far and have already done some bold healing work. Either way, you can gently embrace those fearful inner children and reassure them that they have been very brave.

You may feel out of your comfort zone and uncertain about what to do next. This is normal. For this next part of your journey, your only job is to show up. Be present in the moment and do what is in front of you. An old proverb suggests an approach for attempting audacious things: "All elephants are eaten one bite at a time."

As you progress to the examination of your wound (Step 3), you may feel apprehension, a bit of excitement, or a spark of relief. It's possible you feel all three of those emotions simultaneously. Acknowledging the complexities of your emotions is a sign that you are accessing all of your inner parts. As you seek to understand yourself, you will gain clarity, and your story will unfold in new and surprising ways.

We dance round in a ring and suppose, but the secret sits in the middle and knows.[10]

—Robert Frost

Chapter Two Notes

Step 2b: The Decision to Move Forward

Recognizing and Releasing What Holds You Back

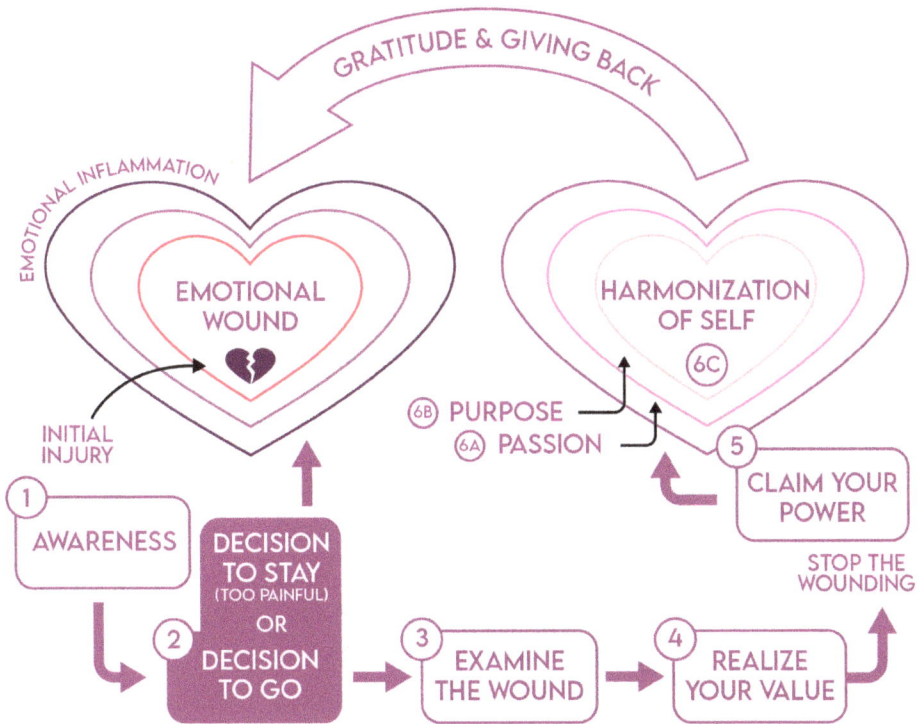

Corbett Model of Emotional Healing & Self-Integration™

Hope and fear cannot occupy the same space.

Invite one to stay.[11]

—Maya Angelou

The ability to love well has been my heart's prayer for many years. Yet, too often, I'm embarrassed by my failure to hit the target of loving my people unconditionally and offering them unrelenting, emotionally healthy support.

I am painfully familiar with the potholes on the path to healthy connections. I have logged many hours there, both on my own journey and with clients who have had the same heartfelt desire to love the people in their lives without fear or reservation.

In our commendable effort to fully connect, we find ourselves tripped up. We run before we walk and often fall short of our desired mark to "do it right this time." The irony is that the greatest stumbling block to authentically loving others well is our inability to genuinely connect with our *own* authentic self and embrace our worth.

How can someone love us if we're a moving target? Most people find that loving themselves is a very high hurdle to clear. Yet, in truth, we can't wholeheartedly love another person with our own fractured heart.

Self-harmonization requires bringing together the fragmented pieces of our being. It begins with our decision to heal. As we become whole, the horizon clears, and we gain clarity to see what our wounded soul could not. We recognize the limitations of our body and intellect, and we are able to experience the Soul Chatter wisdom of our being.

In the previous chapter, we took an honest look at the decision point, the moment in our lives when we consider the personal pain and relationship cost of examining our emotional wound. Step 2a was the decision *not* to examine the wound. Now we'll focus on the choice to overcome those obstacles and move toward healing (Step 2b).

The Decision (Step 2)
Choosing to Pursue Soul Chatter Fluency

Are you ready to let go of the wounds that hold you back? Awesome. Let's chase the life we were meant to live!

The rewards of Soul Chatter fluency are worth facing the inevitable fears. While learning the language of your soul, you will achieve a deep sense of connection with your wild-at-heart and brave, yet wounded, inner children. They've been fighting a difficult battle for a long time, striving to keep the lid on your shame and hurtful memories. Their efforts were often meant to protect you from reexperiencing emotional pain.

In order to pursue your self-harmonization journey in an emotionally healthy way, however, you may find it necessary to re-parent those inner children. It is time for them to learn to work together and be a team. This process will require you to approach life differently and change current patterns and habits.

This is not always easy, as you and your brood have been doing an elaborate dance for a lifetime, and a couple of them are a tad spoiled and used to getting their way. But imagine the joy of accepting yourself—your entire self—and harmonizing your disparate parts into a healthy, confident person.

Visualize that vulnerable, stiff-lipped child who has been brave but scared, as they protect you from a world they perceive will cause an overdose of pain. In your mind's eye, take that terrified inner child onto your lap, look deep into their eyes, and give them the hug that they've been avoiding for most of your existence.

Gently put a hand on either side of their sweet face and console them, "You can play now and quit taking life so seriously. We are okay; the danger is gone." You can confidently assure them that together you can face your truths, identify lies, and be released from the relentless energy it takes to protect the wound that locks away the emotional pain.

As you release your inner children from the burden of guarding your heart, you are free—free to speak your truth, free to fully love, and free to embrace the life you have longed to live.

Intentional Internal Connection
Connecting the Pieces of Me

> Wholeness is not achieved by cutting off a portion of one's being, but by integration of the contraries.[12]
>
> **—Carl Gustav Jung**

There are several therapy modalities devoted to the exploration of our inner parts. Two excellent ones are Dr. Richard Schwartz's Internal Family Systems (IFS) and Dr. Tom Holmes's *Parts Work*.[13] Both therapies embrace the concept that our personality is composed of subpersonalities interacting like a family. Each subpersonality has its own role and set of rules, but their uniting purpose is to protect the core self.

There is a reason our psyche recruits parts of us to guard the vault door of painful memories and perceived shame. Emotional pain is confusing to the intellect, and we don't always know what to do with it, especially when the injury occurs when we are young or in a vulnerable place. So, we push it down and vault it up to be dealt with later, except later never comes up on our calendars. We consciously ignore the emotional beasts, but they wield a great deal of power in our lives and relationships.

As we pursue self-harmonization, our goal is to give a voice to our inner parts and to respect them as contributing members of our whole and balanced being. Internal struggles arise when one of our parts believes its role is the most essential and that it must carry out its self-assigned mission without regarding the other parts. Consider a scenario in which a rogue member of the inner self recklessly eats the entire cake even though the person has a severe gluten intolerance.

In truth, we all have a multidimensional inner being with distinctive and conflicting personas. As we pursue self-harmonization, we will better understand, connect with, and balance our inner parts. That process looks different for every person. The job of parenting our inner children sounds a little fantastical, but it is the best description to understand and achieve self-harmonization.

Note: Do *not* confuse the concept of subpersonalities (used in Parts Work) with dissociative identity disorder, which is a rare psychological disorder that results in the development of multiple distinct personalities. D.I.D. is not at all what we're addressing here.

A Life Story: Letting Go
Thirsting for the Life You Are Drowning In

When Sefora came into my office for her first appointment, she energized the room. "Drakaina energy," she teased. She went on to explain. *Dragon Energy* is slang for a powerful male who is a natural leader, and Sefora was a woman who assuredly projected the yin to the Dragon Energy's yang. She was a woman who leaned in and took control of life. When she spoke, she commanded attention.

It soon became inescapably clear that Sefora was an extreme perfectionist, and she raised the bar even higher by imposing impossible expectations for everything she tackled. During our sessions, I began to suspect that, despite Sefora's meticulously plotted and rigid set of life goals, her authentic aspirations and the persona she projected were at odds.

Her self-perfection was at odds with her rivaling thirst for chaos. When I pointed out that she seemed to have conflicting inner parts, she winced and chirped that it was her way of "avoiding boredom." The previous year she had become a junior partner in a prestigious law firm and was certain that her comfort with chaos and perfection enabled her to remain cool under tremendous pressure. "Maybe that's why the opposing counsel calls me the Ice Queen."

I admired Sefora's spunk and resolve. She confessed that she was determined to live the life her mother and grandmother had dreamt for her. "My mother, Isabella, and my grandma Aba have sacrificed so much so that I could become educated and be successful."

Sefora pursed her lips as she continued, "My mother and father immigrated to the United States from Guatemala with me and my sister when we were very young, always hoping for a better future. Almost as soon as we arrived, my father was killed in an accident at his work. My mother worked every job she could find to support our family, which left little time to spend with us, or on herself. I owe my mother everything."

Sefora had determined that joy was the only acceptable emotion and consequently believed she must always be happy. She experienced extreme anxiety any moment she did not perceive herself to be in a state of bliss. In her mind, any emotion besides happiness was negative and, therefore, unacceptable.

She had disconnected from her inner being and refused to consider her authentic feelings. Furthermore, she had bought into our modern culture's portrayal of a picture-perfect life. It was all recorded on her social media, showing the world a story of her new puppy, romantic dinners, and her spotless apartment.

"I know I *should* be happy," she whispered in my office one day. "Everyone else seems to be. Am I doing something wrong that steals my joy? Why am I so depleted? Maybe I can't do all the things everyone expects of me. Sometimes I don't even want to. My life is so full, there's no time to enjoy it."

Six months into our sessions, Sefora finally confessed that she was wrung out and felt like she was living a robotic existence. "Although I'm smiling in the pictures on my social media, I feel numb and depressed. Perhaps my lustrous life has begun to lose some sparkle."

In our next session, I introduced Sefora to *The Sozo Penny Exercise*. Although simple in nature, it often has a dramatic impact by helping clients visualize the consequences of holding on to what no longer serves them at the expense of what does.

When Sefora arrived, I asked her to put one hand behind her back and to reach the other one out in front of her. I began putting pennies, one at a time, into her outstretched palm. As I placed the coins in Sefora's hand, she named the things that she had been holding on to: a promised partnership, men's approval, her perfectionistic desires. Soon, her hand became full, and the pennies began spilling out.

"I don't think I can hold one more thing in my hand," Sefora giggled.

"That's unfortunate," I smiled. "If you don't put down the pennies, you won't be able to pick up this lovely bracelet." I pointed to the table beside Sefora, where she had accidentally left her bracelet from our last session.

"Now, here is the dilemma: you can't pick up the bracelet with a hand overflowing with pennies. You must make a choice," I told her. "The only way to pick up anything else is to let go of what you're already holding. This is a metaphor for letting go. You can't have what you're longing for when your life is already too full. Putting down what you currently hold creates space and provides an opportunity to receive something new."

"Okay, I get it," she laughed. "It's time to put down the things in my life that are filling up my time and space and requiring all my focus. I need to reevaluate," she said, as determined as ever.

It didn't happen overnight; there were baby steps and missteps. She began by doing what she had gotten really good at—she made a list. This list was of everything that was drowning her.

"I grabbed my journal and wrote down every one of my obligations, promises, and debts. I was determined to address each item and elect to embrace it or remove it from my list. And maybe, more importantly, commit to not adding any further obligations until I can manage the ones I have," she explained.

Over the following months, Sefora examined each of the items on her list, purging many from her life. The ones that remained were those she felt a genuine contentment about.

"My new perspective has gifted me with the presence of mind to realize that my life was so full it was bursting at the seams. At the same time, something vital was missing. I realized that I was reacting, not living. Much of my journey was my attempt to live the life I thought I was supposed to live, not the one I was meant to. I had created a thickly woven web of obligations, debts, and promises. They were noble and sincere, but I was drowning, and my overcommitted life had become a torrid sea of ominous, frantic waves. There was no time for spontaneity, no space for play or balance, not a speck of white space to connect with anyone, especially God."

Sefora re-prioritized and began courageously navigating a journey that was of her own making. As she cleared the obstacles that were obscuring her ability to identify what was most important to her, she was able to embrace her inner children. She was especially sensitive to the grieving little girl who desperately missed her father and was trying to heal the emptiness of his loss for both herself and her mother. That part of Sefora had been running the show most of her adult years.

She began to enjoy a new sense of freedom as she considered her own passions. She was determined to understand what it really meant to live and love well.

"During this time," she reported, "I have gained insight and clarity. I've discovered that, if you define 'all' by the world's terms, you really can't have it *all*. You have to make choices. But you *can* slow down and be grateful for what you *do* have. You can take a deep breath and marvel at how remarkable it is that we live on a dirt clod spinning through space and that every breath we take and every person we love is an unfathomable miracle."

Why We Sabotage Our Own Self-Harmonization

As we get glimmers of the contentment of self-harmonization and begin to experience the joy of being our authentic self, we long to stay in that place of empowerment. We may wonder, "Why do I engage with the things that numb and dissociate me? Why would I be satisfied with being in a state of disconnection and avoid self-harmonization?"

Disconnection serves a purpose, and the methods we choose to disengage and numb ourselves have profound effects on both our lives and the lives of those around us. Bessel van der Kolk, in his book *The Body Keeps the Score*, explains it well:[14]

> The past is alive in the form of gnawing interior discomfort. Their bodies are constantly bombarded by visceral warning signs, and, in an attempt to control these processes, they often become expert at ignoring their gut feelings and in numbing

awareness of what is played out inside. They learn to hide from their selves.

Each of us is aware of the many ways to experience a numbing unawareness. We hide from ourselves—overindulging in eating, drinking, sex, technology, or superficial relationships. Being incredibly busy, isolated, or forgetful can also result in disconnection. There are many ways to identify with our sensations or thoughts and maintain the illusion that we are controlling what we can never control.

In the short term, it might seem easier to numb or disconnect than to choose to pursue the self-harmonization of our inner parts. The impulse to focus on *other* things rather than on our own inner connection is understandable. But this avoidance eventually becomes a habit that is not easily broken. As we disconnect to lessen the pain, our Soul Chatter grows distant and faint.

The motivating truth is that our time on this earth is incredibly short and there is no way to be certain when the melody will stop during our musical-chairs game of numbing awareness. In moments of clarity, we can be certain that we were meant for more than simply indulging our spoiled inner children. It is never too late to be intentional and develop a listening ear to the whispers of our Soul Chatter. We must request that our inner children join us at the negotiating table so that we may wholly pivot toward a life that is authentically satisfying.

Letting Go of the Past for Present-Moment Living

As we form boundaries against outer chaos and quiet the mind chatter, we can connect to the wisdom of our Soul Chatter. The whispers of our soul pierce the constant background noise. It is necessary to let go of the things that hinder us from practicing the present.

We must let go of our childhood to become an adult. We must let go of our bachelorhood to be in a committed relationship. We must let go of our children and allow them to grow up. In the end, we will let go of our earthy life in exchange for something beyond it. Life is a series of transitions, and if we choose to hang on to the past, it will be impossible to fully embrace the now, for now will eventually leave us.

Consider updating your current expectations and routine behaviors to fit present-moment living. Consider the possibility that your modus operandi is getting in the way of your best life. When a door of opportunity opens, you can choose to go through it or not, but do not assume you can always return to the options that are in front of you at this moment. Each moment is an unrepeatable speck in time.

Time-Orientation Awareness: Connecting with the Now

The practice of present-moment living is an essential discipline for overcoming many emotional challenges and cultivating emotional healing. Consider it an Rx for anxiety, overthinking, and a host of mind indulgences. Living in the now is where we lean into authentic life in real time.

We can orient ourselves in three ways with regard to how we experience time: past, present, or future.

Past-Orientation

People who live life with a past-orientation tend to focus on things that have already happened. They may have lingering regrets or a longing for what they once had. The emotions of guilt or depression often accompany past-orientation. A hyperfixation on events from the past can be like a sinkhole, pulling the person into a repeated narrative with ominous images. However, the past cannot be changed; we can only change our view of it. We must be aware of the paralyzing vapors of the past.

Future-Orientation

Stress and anxiety are the most common emotions that accompany future-orientation. Much like the overthinkers in Shakespeare's *Julius Caesar*, who "die many times before their deaths,"[15] the future-oriented person repeatedly imagines dreaded outcomes that may never happen. Living and reliving imaginary outcomes is an emotionally sapping experience, which can even produce physical symptoms such as gastrointestinal distress, heart palpitations, and / or sleep issues.

Present-Orientation

The only time-orientation that allows us to experience real life is the present moment. Being fully present in this exact moment is void of chaos—unless, of course, your room is on fire or someone is screaming at you. There is no guilt or shame of the past and no anxiety or worry about the future. Living in the present is the art of deeply involving yourself in the reality of the life that's in front of you, this very second...okay, *this* second. Did you grab it?

The ability to orient our senses, to richly lean in and experience the present moment, is the best gift we can ever give ourselves. It is a pillar of soul care. The present moment is where we find laughter and peace, and it's where we can experience the presence of God.

The present moment is *not* where we experience dread about the future, and it is *not* the place we wallow in the guilt of events that have already happened. It is the plain old, ordinary *now*, which we may have overlooked in our rush to meet the demands and deadlines in our lives. There are birds chirping, babies cooing, and myriad moments of awe we may be missing. Let's take a moment to breathe and determine to be aware of the life that is unfolding all around us.

Sozo Present Moment Exercise:
Practicing the Present(s)

Conscious Connection

<u>Intention</u>: This is a mindfulness exercise designed to facilitate living in *the now* by holistically orienting your inner being to the present moment and achieving intentional awareness of your senses. Repeatedly practicing this exercise will eventually allow you to access a present-moment orientation whenever you desire it. You can practice present-moment awareness anywhere—at work, at school, or even standing in line at the grocery store.

The purpose of this *Practicing the Present(s)* exercise is to teach sensory awareness, allowing your being to focus on real life in real time. You can intentionally quiet your mind chatter and calm your emotional receptors as you connect with your Soul Chatter.

<u>Side Bonus</u>: The ability to calm your inner core and enter a present-moment orientation is a fantastic practice to pull yourself out of a panic attack.

<u>Materials</u>: A cup of your favorite hot beverage, comfortable clothes, a cozy space, and ten to fifteen minutes of uninterrupted quiet time.

Note: Pre-read these directions so you can fully participate in the process as you experience it.

Instructions:

Lie on a mat or sit on a comfortable chair. Quiet your mind by using the *Basic Connective Conscious Breathwork* method we practiced in Chapter 1. Focus on being aware of your physical body and feel it surrender to the surface you've chosen to sit or lie on.

Once you have oxygenated and energized your conscious centers and are in a relaxed state, explore connections with the outside world by focusing on what is happening around you. Take time to use each of your senses to anchor you in the moment as follows:

Touch: Do a mental body scan. Start at your toes and move slowly to the crown of your head. Ask each muscle, each joint, each area of skin how it feels. Are your clothes tight? How does the chair feel against your skin? Check in with your body and feel what is happening. What is it touching? What temperature is it? Experience the amazing body that's brought you this far on your life's journey. Take a deep breath. Continue to breathe as you mentally scan your body.

Smell: Take another deep breath. This time feel the air going into your nostrils and entering your body. What do you smell? Do you feel the temperature of the air? Breathe in your nose, deep into your gut, and out your mouth. Spend a few moments feeling the calm energy of the oxygen renewing and detoxing your body. Marvel at your sense of smell.

Sight: If your eyes are closed, open them, and appreciate your sense of sight. What do you see? What are the colors? Notice the hues of color around you. Look deeply and appreciate the richness of your environment.

Taste: Continue experiencing the present moment with your sense of taste. If you're lying down, sit up and take a small sip of your beverage. Experience the liquid on your tongue as you drink. Think about the flavor. Does it give you an emotional response? Notice the sensation as the beverage trickles down your throat. Stop, breathe, and appreciate your ability to experience your sense of taste.

Hear: Focus on listening. What do you hear? For a moment, lean into the sounds around you. Hear one sound at a time and you will find layers of sound.

The Takeaway

Lean into the richness of this present moment. With no agenda, ask yourself, "At this very moment, how do I feel?" Take another deep cleansing breath. This is an honest question. How are you feeling currently? Ask your body. Ask your emotions. Ask your Soul Chatter. This is present-moment awareness, and it's helpful for understanding your truth.

Moving Forward and Allowing Emotional Healing

The healing of emotional wounds is much like physical healing; with the proper conditions, a wound will heal. We can set ourselves up for successful emotional healing with good body care: restorative rest, healthy eating, and routine exercise.

In the next section, we will examine our emotional wound—its size, location, and condition—and engage our soul song. We will visualize living an emotionally healed life as we embody our worth and find our voice. The journey continues—and the next step is to proceed to emotional healing by examining our wound (Step 3) and recognizing our value (Step 4).

Chapter Three Notes

SECTION TWO: SOUL SONG

Dancing to the Melody That Emanates from Your Soul

Section Two Letter from Virginia

Hello, Fellow Sojourner!

Soul Song is Section 2 of your Soul Chatter Guide to becoming your best self. This section covers Steps 3 through 5 of the Corbett Model of Emotional Healing & Self-Harmonization™. Here, your intentional journey continues. This section supports you as you bravely examine your emotional wounds and give voice to your inner children, who have been protecting you for a very long time. You'll begin to focus on energizing action for your soul care, a dynamic part of the healing process.

In this *Soul Song* leg of your journey, you will further connect and explore the language of your soul. Consider it the spring cleaning of your inner being—an emotional detox, if you will. Clearing out the toxic energy and opening the windows to your soul will give you the clarity necessary to see through the fog and will allow your authentic self to sit at the head of your family table.

I am excited for you to release your guilt, shame, and fear—and to choose joy. When in doubt, always choose joy!

Be courageous,

Virginia

Section Two Preface

Do you know your soul song?

I have found that each person has a rhythm—a ditty or a tune that emanates from their soul as they experience their authentic state of being. It is lovely to hear a person you adore humming, whistling, or singing their authentic soul song. My great-grandmother had a melodic trill that she breathed in and out, always the same refrain. I smile when I hear my husband's soul song, a happy whistle as he walks in the door.

True confession: my soul song seems to be pop hits from the 1500s. When I'm in the zone, I hum Martin Luther hymns. I know. You heard that right—Martin Luther, the German theologian central to the Reformation. I have no idea why. And that is the point. We do not get to choose our soul song. It's always present and sneaks out the minute we let our guard down and begin to live life.

Our soul song is the energy that hums from our body when we are unabashedly, authentically being the person we were created to be. When we are raw and real, a unique and specific energy comes through us and can burst out in some form of sound—perhaps singing, humming, or whistling.

You will uncover your soul song as you intentionally care for and accept the value of your being. In one instant, it just is. It grows in conjunction with the confidence that accompanies healing and peace.

CHAPTER FOUR

Step 3: Examine the Wound

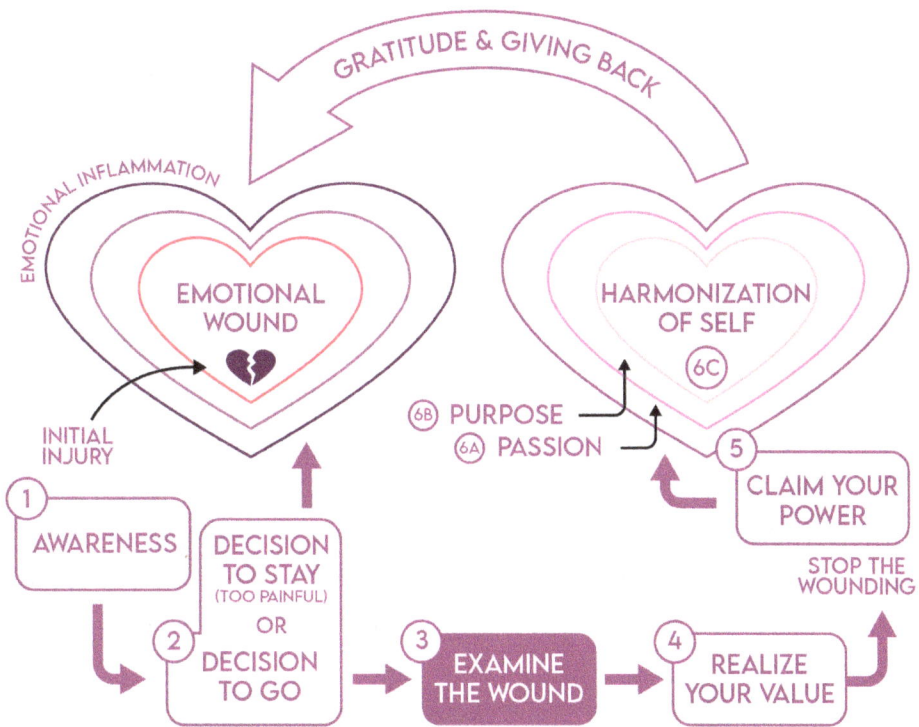

Corbett Model of Emotional Healing & Self-Integration™

A wounded deer leaps the highest.[16]
—Emily Dickinson

Hello there! I am thrilled that you chose to come to this place. Step 3 of the self-harmonization journey is elusive, and it might have seemed as though we would never get here. But here we are, ready to take the next step and embrace the emotional wound we may have been avoiding for most of our lives.

The most insidious quality of an emotional wound is its invisible nature. The people in your life can't always see how much suffering it causes or the burden you are carrying, so the pain often carries a sense of isolation.

How other people perceive your pain neither validates nor negates it. Your emotional wound is yours to experience and define, yours to hold or release. Only you can decide how it will shape you. Examining emotional pain can be lonely. You can do this, though! Just keep trudging forward fearlessly. Your perseverance on this journey is certain to provide new insights. In fact, your pain can lead you to your purpose. But that, too, is yours to choose to recognize.

I suspect that you have coddled and cared for your emotional wound. At other times, you may have despised that part of you. In opposition to your Soul Chatter, your wound has deluded you, has attempted to protect you, and has most likely become a part of you. The dance the two of you have been doing has required a great amount of energy and has altered your life, even if you haven't been aware of its existence.

The chameleon-like nature of the emotional wound makes it difficult to confront, especially when it whispers denials of its very existence. Our emotional wound is the vessel that stores our pain. It may have started with a singular event, but with the progression of time, it has deposited additional memories and introduced new doubts. *Did the injury really happen the way I think it did? Was the aggressor as cruel as I remember?*

Painful memories can be fuzzy, and clarity comes in waves. When it gets difficult, trust your gut. Believe your inner children, and if you feel the journey is getting too painful, do not hesitate to enlist the help of a professional therapist. Talk to several until you find one who is a good fit for you. If you're not certain your therapist is a good fit, they're not. *Persevere.* Allow your soul to sing.

A Life Story: Emotional Wound Examination
Adler's Wings

One of the most profound healing transformations I have witnessed was that of a woman in her midthirties named Adler. Although young, she had an old soul—in part, perhaps, because she had been subjected to extreme abuse throughout her childhood.

Despite having already worked with several therapists, Adler was unable to put together the tangled pieces of her story. She'd never even been able to utter her aggressor's name. She was haunted by horrific nightmares and random flashbacks, both of which were a continuation of the abuse.

As we began working together, Adler drew on her gift of emotional intelligence and addressed her anxiety issues. Over time, she was able to recognize and quash unhealthy generational patterns. She made hopeful progress and was at least able to acknowledge her emotional wound. After several years of diligently working to calm her inner chaos, Adler felt it would serve her well to further examine the emotional wound that had held her back from living the life she knew was meant to be hers.

In one session, I asked Adler if she could visualize the location and state of her emotional wound. She answered without skipping a beat, "Emotional wound? It's as clear to me as if I could see it. It's on my back, exactly where my wings would attach."

The movie *Maleficent*[17] provides a vivid image of a courageous, powerful fairy whose wings have been cruelly hacked off by someone she trusted. Like Maleficent, Adler certainly felt the oppression that tethered her to the ground. Perhaps that is why she had developed such an affinity for feathers. "When I see a feather, it's a reminder that God is in the mix. It's a God-wink," she once mused.

"Can you visualize the wound that's on your back and tell me more about the state it's in?" I pushed further. "Is it bruised? Perhaps it's bloody or scarred over?"

"Yes," she grimaced. "My emotional wound is still a bit bruised—black and green, and tender. In my mind's eye, I picture an embedded rock or a piece of bone that needs to be removed."

Adler's emotional wound had weathered many storms, and she instinctively knew that it was delicate and best left undisturbed. "I would say the emotional wound is located on my back, where it is protected. The pain radiates into my heart.

I'm not sure if this is related, or just an ironic coincidence, but just last week I found a small, physical lump near my heart. I already have an appointment to have a doctor examine that spot and make sure it's nothing serious."

Adler sighed and we both took a deep breath. "Everything is going to work out," she said with a tentative smile.

At our next meeting, I was relieved to see Adler skip into the room. When I asked about her health, she said, "I'm well," in a much lighter tone than she had used in our previous session.

"The lump was benign and quickly removed. You'll love the rest of this story. The technician told me they inserted a tiny piece of metal to mark the location in my breast where the tumor had been. It's called a tumor marker. She said that those metal markers come in literally hundreds of different shapes. Can you guess what shape they had chosen for me?" I smiled at her excitement.

"Wings!" Adler victoriously cooed. "They inserted tiny metal wings that I will have for the rest of my life. I got my wings back! All at once, I feel complete."

The next time we met, we sat on the floor and talked as we worked on a colorful puzzle. Adler reminisced about the pieces of her broken heart and how they fit together. As she revisited random memories and connected them as best she could, she pinballed through the stages of grief—from denial to anger and, ultimately, to acceptance.

The restoration of Adler's wings was more than symbolic. She allowed herself to pivot toward true emotional healing and pictured herself as a victorious warrior. As we worked together, she made great strides beyond her healing journey, carefully collecting tools and techniques to help her cope with anxiety and embrace her worth with self-love.

She was able to consider her fearful, protective, and disconnected inner children, validating and respecting their views. When she experienced horrific, lucid nightmares or persistent fear-thoughts, she could self-soothe and make sense of the experience. After months of courageous work and intentional introspection, Adler surprised herself by recognizing her soul song. "I believe the songbirds trill my soul song. I am energized and delighted when I hear them sing."

In completeness, she was able to refocus her personal energy on her passions. She rediscovered her love of drawing, her art revealing the joy of overcoming pain. A myriad of visions and memories danced onto her canvas. As she claimed her healing victory, her gift of empathy allowed her to help the people who crossed her path with their own restoration.

Adler's journey continues and has gone through several phases. The harmonization of her inner children has provided depth to her character. It is exhilarating to see her life unfolding, guided by the wisdom of an old soul and fueled with freedom. Now she expectantly dances with her passion.

Examination and Care of Your Emotional Wound

Understanding the Four Stages of Healing

Very similar to a physical injury, an emotional wound requires cleansing, removal of debris, and sanitizing in order for it to heal properly. Although it will be part of you for the rest of your life, with conscious effort it can heal, scar over, and eventually be pain-free.

Emotional wounds often remain ignored and neglected. Therefore, acknowledging and caring for your wound by giving it positive and nonjudgmental focus may be exactly what it needs to progress in the healing process.

Stage 1: Stop the Injury

Just like with physical harm, we can't successfully bandage and treat an emotional wound while still being injured. Before we can emotionally heal, the wounding must end. Period. Injured people must remove themselves from the abuse cycle or modify situations and patterns that are emotionally abusive. Stopping a pattern of emotional injury is a very brave thing to do, as it often requires relational cutoffs and intentional life changes.

During the attempt to stop the emotional abuse, it's common for wounded people to question the reality of their circumstances. They may ask, "Is this really abuse or am I overreacting?" The perpetrator may add fuel to those embers of doubt by accusing the wounded of being too sensitive or confused (this is known as gaslighting). Time out! If you're in an emotionally or physically abusive situation, love yourself enough to take time for an honest examination of that relationship.

Stage 2: Acknowledge a Wound Exists

Unlike physical wounds, emotional wounds are insidious and easy to neglect. A gash in your chest would send loved ones rushing for immediate medical attention. Emotional wounds can be just as dangerous (and often more so), but they rarely get the same concern or support. Emotionally wounded people are left to suffer, alone and confused. They may find it difficult to admit the wound exists at all. But the emotional damage remains, and its effects are undeniable.

After years of burying the pain, it can be difficult to give voice to our emotional injuries. There are many ways to conceal a wound so that it goes unnoticed and undisturbed. We may have developed a habit of using sarcasm or aggressiveness to obscure the reality of the pain.

As you begin to examine your wound (no matter how small you believe it is), you must start by acknowledging the reality of its existence and allowing the resultant emotions to surface. This diminishes the wound's power over you, making it possible for you to move forward. Your goal is to reclaim your worth and free yourself of the fear, shame, and guilt that topples future relationships. You deserve to experience the possibilities for love and purpose that await your fully harmonized self.

Stage 3: Contemplate the Location and State of Your Emotional Wound

An unmistakable transformation in the emotional healing process takes place as emotions move from a gut feeling to a mental image to a verbal description. Involving the intellect in the healing process disarms the power of fear. This process intentionally connects the gut consciousness to the mind consciousness.

To develop the mental image of your wound, ask yourself where your emotional wound is located. It can be anywhere on your body. Stop and be gentle with that place on your body as you envision the wound. What is its state? Is it bleeding, scabbed over, or slightly bruised?

When I ask clients about the location and state of their injuries, the certainty of their answers can be striking. They can often point immediately to where their emotional wound is located: "It's right here, above my heart." Or they'll tell me, "It's between my ribs, kind of where my stomach is."

Just as certainly, they can report the condition of their wound: "My emotional wound is tender and bruised." Or they might say, "It's scarred over and has been for some time."

Stage 4: Examine and Cleanse the Emotional Wound

Once you have located your emotional wound and have mentally assessed its state, the next stage is to cleanse it and remove any toxins. It's time to be honest about your condition and acknowledge what has happened. Sometimes it is enough to say it aloud to someone you trust. In therapy, this often sounds like, "I have never said this out loud before, but..." Accept the wound's effect on you and embrace who you are in the process.

To be clear, you do *not* need to recount the details of your trauma (unless you would like to). You just need to be honest about how it affects you and how you would like to process it as part of your story. You can do this with a trusted friend, but consider working with a trained therapist, who can be impartial and guide you through any possible pitfalls that may arise.

This is the part of the journey where you allow your emotional wound to become part of your story, knowing that you may have to wrestle with the reality of past patterns and fears. You can revel in your newly recognized freedom and embrace clarity. You no longer need to avoid your wound—it is an integral part of your identity, having shaped you over the years. You can own your pain on your terms. There is no need to apologize for who you are or to seek anyone's approval to be your authentic self.

Removing Debris

When I was in early grade school, my family lived in the small town of Deaver, Wyoming (we're talking an itty-bitty town). At that time, young ladies wore short dresses and knee socks, but that never stopped us from keeping up with the neighborhood boys when building sagebrush forts or digging holes to China.

My knees were riddled with scrapes and cuts, and to this day, I have the scars to prove it. More times than I care to remember, my grandmother got out her "good tweezer" and magnifying glass to remove gravel and debris from the wounds on my adventure-scarred knees.

In a similar vein, we must get out those good tweezers to remove our emotional debris, but that's a duty almost no one chooses. During the cleansing process, your wounded inner children may try to distract you while they wiggle away. The painful memories of cruel words, rejection, and disappointment are the splinters and pebbles in an emotional wound that fester and prevent true healing. Ignoring our emotional debris by harboring past pain will only cause inflammation, which eventually leads to infection and even more pain.

Sanitizing

Sterilizing a wound is necessary to prevent further infection and initiate proper healing. The process of emotional wound sanitization can look slightly different for each person, depending on the length of time since the injury occurred, the type of wound, and personal resolve. The objective of sanitizing a wound is to provide an opportunity to clear the toxins and enable closure.

For an emotional wound, the sanitizing process reduces or eliminates toxic patterns that may reinfect the injury. It is imperative to disengage from past pain and allow ourselves to engage wholeheartedly in present-moment living. This is how we claim our power back from the wound.

During the sanitization process, the emotionally injured person acknowledges a memory as a calm, rational adult. The perspective of time completes the memory, making it approachable and less foreboding. The memory can be reviewed, reflected on, and refiled in the injured person's brain as a complete story with reformed insight and understanding.

As we process and refile painful memories, we can choose to change our focus to the truth of human frailty and empower our personal growth. We can let go of self-blame or residual shame and give ourselves permission to release pain that may have been blocking joy.

Healing

It's in the nature of wounds to heal. As with physical wounds, our body has a miraculous healing process for our emotional wounds, which begins as soon as we are injured. Our part on the path to restoration is to end any further wounding and to provide an intentional healing environment by incorporating wellness practices. Claiming our victory will empower us to stop unhealthy patterns from creeping back into our relationships.

Note: I want to reiterate that it is *not* necessary to drudge up the details of the injury and relive the pain. We need to allow the emotional wound to heal! What is imperative is that we:

- *Reclaim* the power the pain has stolen.

- *Release* any victimhood that may have energized the wound and given it power to take on a life of its own.

- *Restore* our truth and integrity as we invigorate our life with passion.

The Stuck-ness of a Wounded Place

Being stuck in a wounded place can be a personal hell, even if we're not cognizant of it. Memories of abuse or trauma can be frozen and recorded at their peak, embedding themselves in our network of neurons.

Mentally, we may be stuck at the age or stage of our wounding. As the mental recordings of the trauma run on a continuous loop, our wounded inner children fiercely attempt to repair, relive, and make sense of the lapses in their story.

From the moment of our initial trauma, we may feel as fearful and vulnerable as we did at the time of the injury. In the same way we once feared the monsters under our beds, we may obsess over the terrifying power of our emotional wound. Our fixation simply energizes it and lends it an increasingly destructive sway over us.

The process of dressing our emotional wound is much like pulling off the bedsheets, getting down on the floor, and exposing the monster. This job is usually reserved for brave parents who need their sleep. But now we are the adult. And although the thought of coming face-to-face with the monster that has been haunting our fears and dominating our life shakes us to our core, we can experience a *Wizard of Oz* moment. Like Dorothy, we may come to realize the power that's made us tremble all this time was no more than a weak and flawed human behind a curtain.

Sozo Visualization Exercise:
Examine the Wound (Step 3)

Seeing Past the Emotional Pain

<u>Intention</u>: This is a visualization exercise using explorative meditation to help you become aware of the pain in your body caused by your emotional wound. As you mentally process, you may find it helpful to connect your gut consciousness to your mental consciousness.

<u>Materials</u>: Comfortable clothes and a cozy space. Optional: calming massage oil (lavender, chamomile, tea tree)

<u>Time</u>: 15–20 minutes

Note: Pre-read these directions so you can be present in the process as you experience it. Don't plan anything strenuous after this appointment with self-care.

Instructions:

This is your time to stop, breathe, consider, and practice self-grace. Get a mat, a comfortable lounge chair, or a bed, and nestle into that spot. As you sit or lie down, be aware of your body and feel it surrender to the surface you've chosen.

Begin with connected breathwork from the Sozo Awareness Exercise, connecting your mind, nervous system, gut, heart, and voice.

Inhale: Breathe in through your nose, past your mind center, down your back, following your spine, and fill your gut with clean air.

Exhale: Push the air up the front of your body, past your voice, and out your open mouth.

Do this seven to ten times.

Relax your body and be aware of your breathing and your physical senses. Ask yourself, "Where is my emotional wound?" Take another breath. In the next space of time, be conscious of the first location in your body that comes to your mind.

Imagine your wound. What image do you see? Take another cleansing breath. How does the wound appear to you?

Pay attention to the emotions you're experiencing. Are you feeling fearful or relieved? Or perhaps you feel nothing. As you identify and experience your emotional wound, let it form without trying to force it. Do not get ahead of it. Connect with it as you respect its identity.

Sit with the wound's reality for three to five more breaths.

When you are ready, consider the state of your wound. How old is it? Is it tender to the touch? Ask it what it needs?

Take three to five more breaths.

Place a few drops of massage oil on your hand and consider the story of the wound. As you continue to breathe, take some oil in your hand and massage the area where you perceive the wound to be held.

Breathe, relax, and self-soothe by being present in the moment.

This wound has carried the pain of your emotional injury. As thoughts of the pain go through your mind, do not attach to them. Recognize them and let them flow as if they were traveling by on a river or floating away on a cloud. Do not take this pain back, just be filled with gratitude. The wound was doing its job so that you could do yours. Massage the area around the wound—and the wound itself, if you are comfortable with it.

Take three to five cleansing breaths.

As you breathe deeply, listen for the wisdom of your Soul Chatter. Breathe. Appreciate your magnificent and sophisticated body, how it protects you as it manages your pain.

You are going to be okay. In fact, you are going to be more yourself than you have ever been in your life. But for the moment, give yourself permission to acknowledge and experience what you are feeling. It's okay to cry, to feel confused, or to feel nothing at all. You may be grieving your loss of innocence. Allow yourself to smile or even laugh. You are letting go of the pain that has eluded you. Grief has no expectations or demands. Acknowledge its presence and allow yourself to release it.

Soul Chatter and Emotional Energy

Tender-to-the-Touch Avoidance: Becoming Friends with Your Emotional Beast

As we choose to become fluent in our Soul Chatter, we will experience the connection of our consciousness centers and give voice to the emotional energy residing within our wound. As we intentionally acknowledge the wound we have been harboring, there is always the possibility it might growl at us for attempting to tap into buried memories.

Navigating uncharted emotional territory may trigger unfinished business that has been trapped in our subconscious. We may instantly become fearful or angry as we grasp for control. Recognize this reaction for what it is: our psyche's attempt to protect our emotional wound by making it uncomfortable to explore.

On some level, your inner children believe the pain is too great to unleash. You might have spent years setting up schemas designed to avoid addressing the feelings around the memories. Remember, you are strong and brave and your authentic self is worth fighting for. Be aware of your Soul Chatter as it informs your journey.

Note: As with each step in the healing process, if you are feeling emotionally queasy, do not hesitate to enlist support or reach out to a professional therapist.

Coping Mechanisms
Choosing Healthy and Replacing Not-So-Healthy

At this stage, it is natural to either fight the flood of energy-charged emotions, freeze and feel nothing, or flee by disconnecting and detaching. We might be tempted to turn toward go-to coping mechanisms, such as grabbing the vodka, calling for a pizza, or punching a wall. Understand that these impulses are our inner children rallying to obtain a feeling of control or hiding from what they fear.

It will be helpful for our long-term emotional and physical health if we can nip those potentially unhealthy coping mechanisms in the bud. We can anticipate them and intentionally move toward positive substitutions, such as meditation, prayer, exercise, talk therapy, gardening, creating, or journaling.

The energy of our emotions is powerful—we can choose to allow that energy to run wild, or we can use it productively and creatively. Healthy coping mechanisms are a way of harnessing emotional energy.

As you become fluent in your Soul Chatter, you can be mentally clear about what is happening. And as you visualize your emotional beast and learn your patterns, you can be less fearful. You will no longer need to avoid the thought of the memory. It's a lot like taming a wild horse. Your dialogue with your emotional pain may sound something like this: "There you are. I recognize that pain-memory. You don't need to be so prickly. We are okay now."

Respect, hear, and soothe. In time, it is possible to befriend, re-parent, and harmonize your emotions. Harnessing your Soul Chatter and using your emotional energy positively is your personal power for creating the story you were meant to live.

Healing Grace

Examining the Wound (Step 3) is an evolving process. As we boldly and confidently shed each toxic layer of residual emotional pain, new insights will be revealed and secondary injuries may become apparent. But you are different now. You understand the process and appreciate any newfound clarity. Each layer shed will reduce your emotional baggage and enable a deeper soul-level connection. Take heart—claim your victory. This time you are ready.

As we continue the soul song phase of our Soul Chatter journey, the next chapter will cover *Realizing Your Value* (Step 4). In this step, we will learn to accept our worth and revel in our uniqueness. But before we go there, take a moment to claim your victory.

Well done. Allow yourself a safe space to take an energizing breath and delight in a place of calm. It is my sincere hope that you are wiggling your toes and smiling as you feel immense love and claim the joy of being you.

Chapter Four Notes

CHAPTER FIVE

Step 4: Realization of Value

Discovering Your True Worth

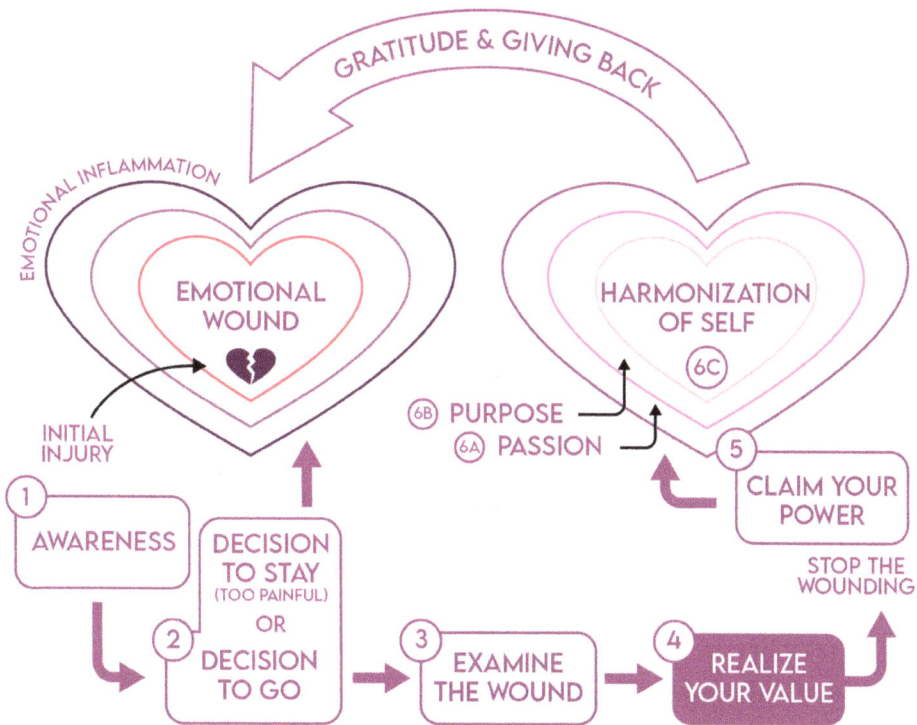

GRATITUDE & GIVING BACK

EMOTIONAL INFLAMMATION

EMOTIONAL WOUND

INITIAL INJURY

HARMONIZATION OF SELF

6C

6B PURPOSE
6A PASSION

1 AWARENESS

DECISION TO STAY (TOO PAINFUL) OR 2 DECISION TO GO

3 EXAMINE THE WOUND

4 REALIZE YOUR VALUE

5 CLAIM YOUR POWER

STOP THE WOUNDING

Corbett Model of Emotional Healing & Self-Integration™

True humility is not thinking less of yourself; it is thinking of
yourself less.[18]
—Rick Warren

At this very moment, right where you are, you are complete. I know all the improvement projects you long to make. I understand the if-onlys you feel are essential to your happiness. The truth is that you don't have to *do* anything to be who you're meant to be. You already are.

There, I said it. The waves of doubt flood your mind, lying to you about your worth. You may choose to spend your whole life focusing on your *perceived* flaws instead of reveling in your unique gifts. You may believe the lies that people have told you—like those who say you must transform yourself to be acceptable, who say you must climb the next mountain in order to be valuable.

The widest chasm in the universe is the distance between who we are and who we believe we ought to be. There is nothing that grieves me more than a life of unrealized possibilities—the plays unwritten, the bread unbaked, the love not received.

The irony of atrophied potential is that the root cause is always the same. We feel the human need to produce something of value, but because we believe the lie that our worth is based on our performance, we feel too unworthy to employ our unique gifts, which is precisely what's needed to create anything of value. In other words, our inability to recognize our value saps us of the creative energy needed to pursue our true passions and live an authentic life.

We swim daily in beach-ready, hyper-filtered images—real and figurative. The world is a fickle place. Culture changes like the ocean tide. Basing our worth on the opinions of other people is a no-win strategy that will eventually bring us crashing back to a rocky shore.

Can you imagine a butterfly that sits on a flower and never flies? Suppose it spent its entire butterfly-life staring at a spot on its wing, believing itself too flawed to do exactly what it was put on earth to do. We do that. We fixate on the spot on our wings and never use our perfect wings to take flight.

If we could view the beauty of our souls, then our flaws would pale in comparison. So often, instead of soaring, we choose to pick up the mental magnifying glass and focus on our faults until we can see nothing else. This drains us of the energy it takes to live out who we are meant to be.

I have spent thousands of hours counseling people who are evolving butterflies, but only a few have ever chosen to use their gorgeous wings. Internalizing value is a long process for some and a sudden revelation for others. But it is possible to courageously refocus on the joy and beauty of your life, spread those spotted wings, and soar.

Sozo Mini Exercise:
Value (Step 3)

Bill-ieve

A Conceptual Exercise to Internalize Value

<u>Materials</u>: A paper currency bill (the largest denomination you have) and a sense of adventure.

Pick up your paper bill and look at it. Notice the denomination of the bill. How much is it worth? We know its worth because the value is printed right on the surface.

Now, take it and wad it up. Really, crunch up that money. (You may feel uneasy doing this, but consider it therapy.)

Next, let's get a little crazy...

Throw it on the floor and step on it. You can even jump on it!

Now, rescue that bill from the floor and take a good look at it. Notice the value of the bill. Has it changed? Or is it still the same amount?

You have a lot in common with that money. The bumps and bruises you experience in life may weaken you and shake your confidence. You can get stepped on, rolled around, and banged up, but your true, God-given worth never changes. The value of your being cannot be diminished—no matter what your circumstances or outside forces attempt to convince you otherwise.

A Sozo Value Story: Accepting the Cost
If a Soul Felt Its Worth

In the late spring of her fortieth year, Ani set an intention to become herself. She strutted into my office and flashed a confident smile. Over the past several years, I had accompanied Ani on her healing journey in our work together.

Ani's story was one of childhood trauma and the terror of abandonment. As the daughter of an abusive, self-absorbed mother and an absent father, she experienced the ripping open of her emotional wound repeatedly. Over and over, as it began to heal, it would be reinjured at critical times throughout her formative years.

She spent her childhood longing to have a storybook connection with either parent, and she blamed herself for feeling isolated. In her teenage years, she attempted to fill the void with sex and drugs. That period of her life produced its own regret, which added to the toxic energy of her inner child. Ani's most prevalent childhood memory was being told that she was a "worthless, abysmal failure."

"There was almost a comfort to being pronounced worthless early on in my life; it took the pressure off," she explained. Ani adopted and retooled those hateful words into a single self-mantra, an inner voice constantly reminding her, "You are unlovable. Everyone you care about will abandon you and you will end up alone."

Her mother fed that narrative by constantly questioning Ani's character and telling her that she would never be a wife or mother. This projection proved to be incorrect when twenty-one-year-old Ani hooked up with Hank, the office heart-throb, at their company Christmas party. The intensity of their connection advanced to a cyclonic courtship and a quick trip to the altar three months later.

"Life was good—really good. I finally felt the connection I had longed for my entire life. Hank and I were invincible. We had crazy-fun in those early years. And what do you know? We had four children by our fifth anniversary. That early period of our marriage required most of the energy either of us had," Ani reminisced.

The more demanding life became, the more distant Hank seemed. As Hank retreated, Ani catastrophized and did her part to push him away. "In all honesty, to protect my emotional wound, I think I subconsciously felt it would be easier for me to force him to leave than to experience the pain of him abandoning me," she continued. "In my effort to push him away, I was mean. How much sense does that make? Pushing someone away so they don't leave you?"

Ani was in a fear pattern. She would grow cold, push Hank away, and then endeavor to make up. She swore to stop the behaviors. But this pattern became the norm in Ani and Hank's household and continued to escalate.

One cold winter night, after nearly fifteen years of marriage, the thing Ani considered to be inevitable did indeed happen. After a horrible fight, Ani told Hank to leave and never come back. He obliged and left for the last time. That was the week Ani decided to reassess her life and do things differently. That was the week she became my client.

In our first session, she expressed how devastating it was to have her fear of abandonment realized. "I waited for Hank to walk in the door all night. I didn't sleep. I lay alone in the dark, staring at the ceiling. My chest pounded so hard I thought my heart had exploded. I always knew this would happen. My greatest fear of being alone is now what I am living out. My mother told me many times throughout my life that I was a 'damn loser and no one would ever want me.' I hated that she was right; I *am* worthless."

Ani was low, very low. But she took a deep breath and rallied. "I am a lot of things, and one of them is a fighter. I know that I do not quit. But I also have no idea what to do next, so that's why I'm here."

It took months of hard work for Ani to get to a place where she was comfortable enough to examine her emotional wounds. She began listening to her *Soul Chatter* to understand how her authentic self connected to the "loser" persona that had been assigned to her.

During therapy, Ani talked openly and matter-of-factly about the painful experiences of her childhood (some of them for the first time out loud). She refiled her tender childhood memories through the lens of an adult instead of through the hazy lens of an abandoned little girl.

She identified patterns, behaviors, and defense mechanisms that had once served her well but were now sabotaging current relationships and blocking her from being her best self. She worked to replace her toxic thought patterns with positive affirmations instead of the fear-based lies that had echoed in her head for years.

For one session, I asked Ani to bring a picture of herself as a child. She handed me a photo of a little blue-eyed girl and excitedly told me all about the sweet child in the picture. "She is the cutest little girl with a wrinkled-up nose," she smiled, as she described herself. "See her plaid dress and the band-aid on her knee? She got that from running as fast as she could. She is whimsical and ornery. She is adventurous and loves the grass beneath her feet and her stuffed cat, Grover. She adores life and is ready to scramble down the sidewalk to embrace it. I like this little girl."

With a tilted head, I asked, "That whimsical, ornery little girl who embraces life and loves her blue stuffed cat—how do you feel about her and what do you think she deserves in this life?"

"She deserves the best," Ani blurted. "She should be cared for and loved because she is precious."

Our eyes met. She was finally ready to *hear* what I was about to say. "Ani, that little girl—the one who loves the grass beneath her feet and running as fast as she can—she *is* you. You are responsible for her destiny. You should be valued, cared for, and loved because you are so precious. You are whimsical and worthy, and you deserve to be treasured."

I was only telling her what she already knew to be true. Ani took in a deep breath as the fog lifted. She carried the picture home with her, thinking deeply on the value of Little Ani.

When Ani returned to my office the following week, she was excited to talk about what had been going on in her life. She'd had a eureka moment, and her eyes were filled with tears as she shared, "After the initial uneasiness, I gave myself over to the moment. In real life, in real time, I experienced being present in the now. I felt connected in a powerful way. I meditated, prayed, and let go of a lot of hurt. For the first time, that void in me was filled, and I fully internalized my value. From the depth of my being, I knew the author of love saw me as a creation of His perfection."

I smiled at Ani and noticed that she physically looked like a different person. She glowed as she continued, "I tried to recover my breath as I felt the lifelong fear in me drift away. With a certainty I had never felt before, I *knew* God adored me as I was—right at that moment."

Ani paused, then slowly continued, "Now that I have experienced unconditional love, everything else on this earth pales in comparison. I have come face-to-face with Grace. My value is secure, and nothing can change that—nothing. Not the opinion of my parents, not Hank, not my coworkers—no one can take away my value. No human can make me less."

Up till now, Ani had been searching for an assurance of her value from the people in her life. She had based her self-worth on the kudos of her family, friends, colleagues, and neighbors in an effort to fill a hole in her soul. The problem with this hole-of-need is that it is actually a bottomless pit. The energy to fill it becomes an all-consuming, self-centered, and addictive effort.

Once Ani's recognition of her worth took root, some things that she had allowed in her life were no longer acceptable to bring into her new chapter. She began making small changes in her perspective and her behaviors.

"I am the person I have always been. I refuse to apologize for that anymore. For years, I have been a strong woman. This makes some people uncomfortable, and they try to push me down. In the past, when I sensed their discomfort, I would shrink back. I have spent too many years hiding my strengths and abilities and trying to compensate for them. Some of the people in my life have attempted to make me feel shame. I am done walking on eggshells and modifying my persona to make them happy. I have decided to quit hiding and to embrace my authentic life. I choose to be the author of my own story."

As Ani spoke, her voice had a firm, regular cadence, and her face was relaxed. She was taking a victory lap on her emotional healing journey as she internalized her value.

Being assured of her value (Step 4), Ani ventured to the next step of Soul Chatter fluency, *Finding Your Inner Voice* (Step 5). It was thrilling to hear Ani courageously begin to verbalize her feelings and enact protective boundaries in her relationships.

She understood the power of saying what she means and developed techniques to kindly, but assertively, say no when she needed to. I was delighted to see her blossom, to see her value herself enough to let go of the guilt of not performing to other people's expectations.

We innately understand the need to protect and value the vulnerable, but we often lose sight of the need to protect and value ourselves. We can recapture lost or unrealized passions as we live into our value and find our *Soul Chatter* message. Ani's story is one of hope. As long as we are alive, there is always hope.

Practicing Self-Grace

How can we expect the people in our lives to love us and treat us with respect if we believe we are not lovable and do not respect our being? Many of us could benefit from the habit of mindfully treating ourselves with the care we would extend to someone we love. In this next Sozo exercise, we will practice techniques to connect with our younger selves and appreciate the care and grace we can give to further their future.

Sozo Memory Exploration Exercise:
Reprocessing Your Negatives

A visual exercise for regaining a sense of self—Part 1

<u>Materials</u>: Favorite photo of you as a child.

<u>Note</u>: This exercise can be done alone or with a trusted friend. Find a favorite photo of yourself as a young child. What you are doing in this photo is not as important as your feeling of connection to the child you see in the picture.

Step 1:

Find a safe space where you can relax and not be interrupted.

Begin by doing the *Connective Conscious Breathwork* exercise we learned in Chapter 1. Take seven to ten deep cleansing breaths. Connect to your consciousness and lean into the present moment. Breathe in through your nose and trace the air past your mind consciousness and down the back of your spine. Let it fill your gut consciousness. Release the breath up the front of your body, past your voice consciousness, and out your mouth.

Once you feel present, pick up the picture from your childhood. (Take your time and remember to continue breathing.)

Take a look at the photograph and be aware of your feelings. Scan the picture and imagine what the small child in the photo is thinking and feeling. Try to connect with that child as if she were in the room with you. What are your feelings as you look at her? Do you feel protective? Do you think she has potential to do great things?

Put down the photo. Take another deep conscious breath. Allow time to fill any void that separates you from the small child in the picture. Surrender to unconditional love and positivity.

Step 2:

Pick up the picture again. This time, take note of things you may not have noticed before. Look at the background. Are there any people present with the child in the picture? Study the child's expression.

What is she wearing? Consider what she may feel at that moment. What do you wish for her? What do you wish for her future? What would you do to help her if you could? What would you say to her? What do you think about the value of that child?

Put down the photo. Take another deep connecting breath. Assess how you are feeling at this moment. How do you feel physically? Does any area of your body come to mind? What is the sensation you feel?

Accept how you feel and don't fight to change it. Try to sit with these feelings. Take a break. Relax. Smile.

Step 3:

Put the picture in a place you will see every day—maybe a bathroom mirror, your car, or a desk. When you see the picture, think of this child's value and your dreams for this child.

Negative thoughts about the child are negative thoughts about yourself. As this child has grown and become who you are today, she is no less valuable. You are responsible for making sure this child is encouraged and validated in order for her to live her best life.

Excavating Your True Self

You have most likely heard the story of the older brother whispering to his new-born baby brother, "Quick, tell me everything before you forget." There is a lot of truth in the older brother's desire. Shame, guilt, and blame get layered on as they cast a shadow over our once carefree self. In this next exercise, we will explore ways to recapture the ease of being our authentic self.

Sozo Exercise:
Affirming Our Inner Children

A visual exercise for identifying negative self-talk—Part 2

<u>Materials</u>: Favorite photo of you as a child, a journal, and a pen.

<u>Note</u>: Return to the photograph of yourself as a child from the previous exercise, or you can choose another photo that has meaning to you. Again, it is not as important what you are doing in the picture as how you feel about the child in the photo. It should be a picture that you feel positive about and can connect with.

Step 1:

Find a place where you will not be interrupted. Begin by centering yourself with consciousness connection breathwork. Breathe in through your nose and out through your mouth.

Pick up the picture and gaze at it. Imagine this child sitting beside you and looking up to you with big curious eyes. How do you feel about this child? What would you say to her? Would you shame or encourage her?

Put down the photo. Take a deep breath as you balance your thoughts and your emotions.

Step 2:

Next, take a moment in silence as you Soul-Chatter-connect with your being. Do you typically judge and criticize yourself, or do you encourage yourself with self-talk? What are the phrases you currently use in your self-talk? Do you have a negative mantra you tell yourself? A positive one? Where did those mantras come from?

Take another deep breath.

Step 3:

Once again, pick up the photo and gaze at the child. The negative mantra you say to yourself, you are also saying to her. What could you say instead?

Complete the following statements in your journal.

Baby steps are important. What is something you can do to give grace to your inner children? Fill out this sentence to take a small action toward self-grace.

I will commit to being true to who I am and honoring my own needs by

_____ even if it makes someone (or myself) un-comfortable.

I *know* my worth and will be aware of self-criticism and negative self-talk. I will change the negative mantra that I have been using from

_____ to

_____ so I can be gentle and treat my inner children with the love they should have.

I give myself permission to _____ in order to explore my passions.

Step 4:

Pick up the photo one last time and share your plan with the small child by reciting the above commitments and telling her how you are taking steps to value her. Give yourself a hug. (Really! Take both arms, embrace your body, and squeeze!) You have been brave and have done a wonderful job valuing both your child self and your future self.

Valuing Our Authentic Selves

As we honor and care for ourselves, we set the bar and teach others how to treat and respect us. A lifelong habit of treating ourselves poorly—of doubting our abilities and putting our own needs behind every other priority—may have become a habit we no longer notice.

If you've developed this habit, begin treating yourself the way you wish to be treated—not by indulging your whims but by respecting your being. Learn to self-regulate by quieting your mind chatter, balancing your emotions, and connecting with your Soul Chatter. This is not an overnight process, but you can rely on the truth that the same determination and grit that has gotten you to this point will see you through the next leg of your journey. Here are some helpful practices to reinforce your progress:

Be kind to yourself and appreciate the person you are right at this moment. As you begin to practice emotional self-care, be conscious of any negative mantras you have developed. Recognize them for what they are—a way that you perpetuate self-abuse. Tell yourself to stop (out loud, if you can).

Rewrite those negative mantras! Destructive self-talk and neglecting our own needs are habits that need to be broken. Keep positive counter-mantras written on a card or in your phone so they can become as automatic as your destructive self-talk used to be.

Baby steps! It's okay to crawl before you run. Awareness of your worth may seem like an unrelated concept on the journey to becoming fluent in your Soul Chatter. However, everything that follows hinges on this truth. Enjoy the freedom of knowing your value is not based on the accolades of another human, and you don't need permission to be the person you have always been.

Worth is outside of time. You aren't finished baking yet. Your self-harmonization journey is bold and beautiful, and you will never be the same (nor will you want to be). Understand that your journey is a process, and the beauty of who you are is unveiled in this process. There is no rush. The only urgency ought to be the excitement you feel as you allow yourself to experience life exactly as it should be lived.

Moving Forward

In the next chapter ("It's All Relatives"), we will consider the dilemma of honoring our own worth when it seems to conflict with loving the people in our lives. (I promised we would deal with the realities and complexities of our relationships!) We will explore family dynamics and other-sabotage.

But for this moment, stretch out your arm in front of you. Gaze at your hand. Consider the lives this hand has touched—the hands it has held, the shoulders it has patted with reassurance. Consider the experiences it has had and what it is capable of. Thank you for being you, for what you have done and what you will do. Hold your hands, massage them, appreciate them. Appreciate *you*.

Chapter Five Notes

CHAPTER SIX

Conquering Challenging Relationships
It's All Relative

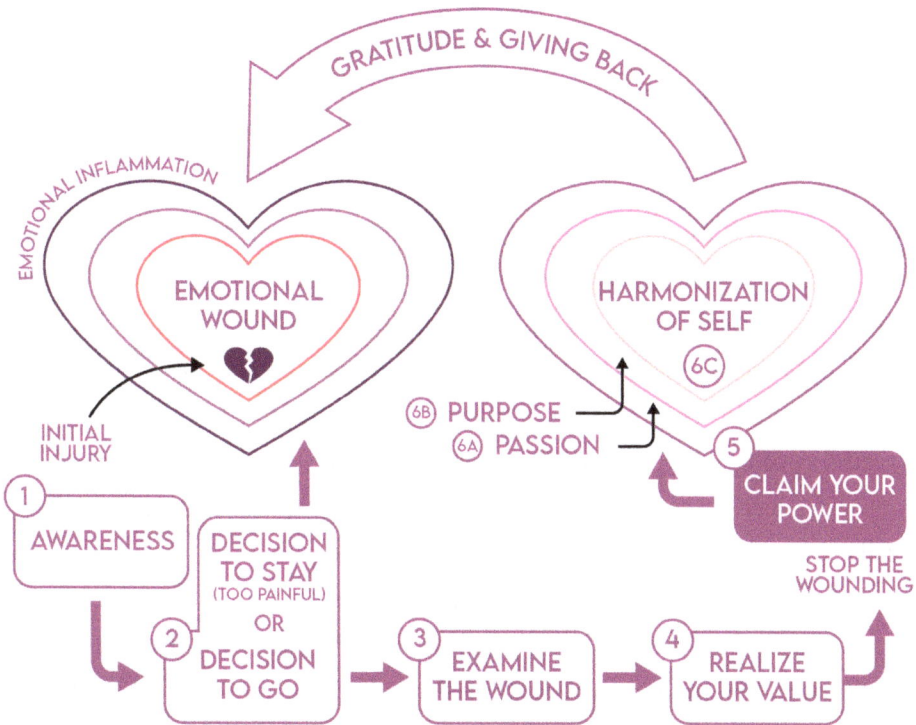

Corbett Model of Emotional Healing & Self-Integration™

> Feelings of worth can flourish only in an atmosphere where individual differences are appreciated, mistakes are tolerated, communication is open, and rules are flexible—the kind of atmosphere that is found in a nurturing family.[19]
> —**Virginia Satir**

The Dilemma
Developing Self and Loving Our Heart-People Well

Do you desire unconditional love—at the very least, to love and be loved in an emotionally healthy way? Oh my, I'm already compromising on the conditions of unconditional love. By its nature, it has *no* conditions. Period. We love and are loved, simply for who we are.

Many of us have a great desire to love our heart-people well, yet we rarely hit that mark. We struggle with the consequences of burdening our relationships with conditions and agendas. That is what makes *unconditional* love so very difficult to bestow or obtain, even though it's life changing when we give or receive it.

Love might ask that we wash the feet of the one who just stepped on our dream. The self-sacrifice required to offer complete grace to a flawed human exposes us to the possibility of being wounded. The most courageous act on our emotional healing journey is the decision to risk being vulnerable again—vulnerable enough to love and live well.

Extending grace to the people in our life, while also maintaining the sacred personal space needed to energize our Soul Chatter, is necessary for the journey to self-harmonization. We can accomplish this balanced dichotomy only when we remain vulnerable enough to connect to others while maintaining healthy boundaries. A great deal of awareness and personal energy is required to be other-centered and simultaneously self-aware.

Human imperfection guarantees that none of our relationships will ever be flawless. In fact, as we bump through our journey, we *will* wound the very people we are trying to nurture, and they will hurt us as well. That is why forgiveness and intentional grace is the foundation for every healthy long-term relationship.

As we choose emotional wellness and the path toward self-harmonization, we will be drawn in by positivity, gratitude, and creative energy. At the same time, negativity, destruction, and toxic energy will repulse us. We will crave and strive for higher ideals and purpose. Being in tune with Soul Chatter clarity will lead us to our passions and allow us to have the confidence to pursue our uniqueness.

During this process, it's imperative that we prepare for the reality that some of our key people may not be supportive. They may push back against the inevitable changes we will need to make.

We can take the hard-sought, less-traveled road to becoming our best self, but it is not fair to expect the people in our lives to always be in lockstep with us. Many times, loving *both* ourselves and our people well while pursuing our journey requires us to respect their rejection of our choice even as we move toward self-harmonization (perhaps without their support).

They may insist on trying to hinder our journey because they are not comfortable with our aspirations. If they refuse to give us the space and grace we need to follow our hearts, we may be forced to make a difficult choice: to let go of our personal goals or to modify our relationship.

This can be a gut-wrenching choice, and many people turn away from their own journeys at this point or spend years delaying a decision they will never make. People struggling with their choices can devote hundreds of hours of therapy to this exact dynamic.

To be clear: our decision to seek self-harmonization ultimately carries a cost. If we pursue the life that beckons us, we may lose a current relationship or an accustomed lifestyle. On the other hand, we risk losing our passions, possibilities, and our authenticity if we do not. Either way, it is important to understand that the doors of opportunity are time sensitive and can close at any moment. Authentic opportunities are present-moment chances, and the one in front of you may never come again.

A Sozo Healing Story:
Marthafern

When my mother was nine years old, she woke up in the back of the family station wagon, the sunrise peeking through the trees, as she and her family crossed a bridge entering the city of Cheyenne, Wyoming. Instantaneously, she realized three things: it was morning, her family was returning home to Sheridan, and her father had died.

Her world had shattered. The man who adored her, made her laugh, and confirmed her unconditional worth would never come home again. She had never experienced this horrific feeling: completely isolated, hopeless, and abandoned, cut off from everything and everyone.

She was no longer the apple of someone's eye, no longer the little girl who could twirl into her daddy's heart. Her fun-loving buddy was gone, and the world had crumbled. The message she received was forever etched in her soul: "Marthafern, you are nothing. You have no worth, and whatever you do will fail."

Those words must be truth, she thought. *I'm not even important enough to be woken up and told my daddy has died on the operating table during his open-heart surgery.*

That moment in time would be forever frozen in my mother's mind. There she was, stuck. She would grow and mature physically into adulthood, but she would never completely mature emotionally. For the rest of her life, a part of her would always be an abandoned nine-year-old.

My mother was a complex person, a dichotomy—at times, she was a wise, Yoda-esque, old soul, but at other times, she was impetuous and childlike. As her eldest daughter, I was left in the complicated position of having to parent my own mother at times.

She was silly and creative and had the most raucous laugh I have ever known. But ultimately, when she wanted her way, she'd play the trump card and say, "Because I'm your mother, that's why." So, she always got what she wanted.

Our home, filled with creativity and chaos, was a roller-coaster ride of conflict, extreme emotion, joyous fun, and waves of pain. As a result, so were our relationships.

In the wee hours one morning of my sixth-grade year, my mother shattered the garage door backing out her car, gun in hand, threatening to commit suicide. I tried to stop her from leaving, even running behind the car, but I wasn't successful. Several long hours later, she returned home. That was one of the happiest and angriest moments of my life. She handed me the gun and told me to get rid of it. I hid it behind the wall insulation in our unfinished basement, where it stayed for some time.

Going forward, my mother would wax and wane. At times, she was brilliant; at others, she shut down. She would emotionally disappear, retreating into her bedroom to read romance novels. Stacked like cordwood against her bedroom walls, reaching the ceiling in some places, they were her way to escape reality, to numb the wound. There are worse ways to numb out, but I still hate those damn books.

When she wasn't numbing, she was producing. In "production mode," my mother didn't pussyfoot around. There are small, well-run factories that couldn't have kept up with her output.

I remember the year that Care Bears were extremely popular and almost impossible to buy. My mother decided to make a complete Care Bear set for every child she knew. She made over one hundred of the brightly colored bears. For the better part of the summer, the living room was ankle deep in Care Bear fur and stuffing. The bears were wonderful and produced the desired effect of laughs and smiles. I marveled at my mother—the huge mess, the wonderful bears, and the balance between production and chaos.

Another time this pattern played out was right before my wedding. My husband and I had a two-year engagement, which was an exercise in extreme patience, to say the least. The benefit to long engagements (if there is one) is that you have time to plan, really plan. This equates to getting married roughly forty-five thousand times in your head.

I had our wedding day imagined, down to the most minute detail. I found a lovely, yet expensive, wedding dress that I adored. I was sure my life wouldn't be complete if I didn't wear it. I was telling my future mother-in-law how wonderful *the* dress was when she asked me if I would rather wear *her* dress. *Ahhhhh, no, not really*, I thought, *but I had better smile and be agreeable.*

How was I going to get out of this? She ran to her basement and brought back what turned out to be the most beautiful dress I had ever seen. "Yes, I would. I would love to wear your dress," I said.

Having had my soon-to-be mother-in-law entrust me with her thirty-three-year-old wedding dress, off I went to consult with my own mother, who could make any necessary alterations. We excitedly put the dress on me and went to zip it up. Have you ever had one of those moments when you desperately wanted something to work but there was no way it was going to?

Try as we might, we could not pull the antique fabric around my chest to zip the wedding dress together. Suddenly, the scene went into slow motion as my mother grabbed her "good Gingher scissors" and slit the dress right up the front. My heart literally stopped.

"Mom! You just cut the front of my future mother-in-law's dress! This is not the best way to start a long and positive relationship." I panicked. *Breathe, breathe, breathe.*

Undeterred, my mother continued with her seamstress brilliance. She reached around to the back of the long dress train and trimmed off a perfectly fitting piece of fabric, shaped and beaded it, and made a placket for the front of the dress that exquisitely covered the alteration. She then beaded the entire dress with swirls of pearlescence. It was flawless.

In her usual style, my mother had tapped into her creative genius and made the revamped dress even more beautiful than it had previously been. It was an amazing feat. On our wedding day, the gorgeous dress and the history behind it astonished everyone, including me and, more importantly, my new mother-in-law.

Complicated relationships and complex family dynamics were hallmarks of my childhood. My mother was a passionate person, who deeply loved the people in her life. She was the most talented woman I'd ever met, with the most untapped potential you could imagine. She was confident and wise beyond her years, but also demanding and insecure. She was and she wasn't, all at once.

My mother passed away at sixty-seven years young. At the early stages of my grieving process, I used to wonder what she might have accomplished if she had healed from her childhood emotional wound and lived into her potential. But in time, I understood that I was trying to examine my mother's life on my terms, and that is not fair to her.

Loving my mother well required giving her space and respecting that the choices she made in her life were hers to make. She lived a passionate, turbulent life, and she spent tons of money on craft supplies. Those are a few things that made her unique, quirky, and so very full of life. Those are also the pieces of her that shaped me into the person I am today.

Most of my childhood, I felt like a moth dancing near a chaotic flame. At times, I fanned the flame; at others, I distanced myself from it. At some point, I began to see the flame as separate from myself and even from my mother. It's the fire of the generational pain we wrestle to break away from. I began wanting to free the people I loved from the allure of it. In response, I've dedicated my life to doing just that, not just for my own family but for all wounded people.

As humans, we all wrestle with the deep-rooted, alluring flame of seductive impulses and generational patterns. In order to achieve Soul Chatter fluency on our journey to self-harmonization, we must differentiate what is uniquely us and what is an assigned narrative from our family system.

You carry the torch of the love, relationships, and generational patterns that may have been passed down to you, but they do not need to define you. This is *your* life, and you can choose to write your story on your terms with your unique panache.

Writing Our Own Stories

In our lifelong effort to seek connection and win validation, our family of origin plays a key role and sets the agenda from the outset. We rely on them to help us find who we are. They help us discover our worldview and navigate the traits we've inherited.

Murray Bowen, one of the founders of Family Systems Theory, observed, "The basic building blocks of a 'self' are inborn, but an individual's family relationships during childhood and adolescence primarily determine how much 'self' he develops. Once established, the level of 'self' rarely changes unless a person makes *a structured and long-term effort to change*" (emphasis mine).[20]

That is what self-harmonization (Soul Chatter fluency) requires—a structured and long-term effort to examine our family system's rules and possibly to transition from the role we were assigned in our childhood into an adult role of our choosing.

We commonly accept our assigned role as unalterable truth without questioning its narrative. This dynamic is often the stumbling block to embarking on our own self-harmonization journey.

In order to live as self-actualized adults, we must embrace the responsibility we have to both ourselves and our descendants, respecting our inheritance while also deliberately claiming our personal power and releasing generational pain and unhealthy relationship patterns. To do this, it is helpful to recognize other-sabotage and the dynamics of the family system.

Sozo Exercise:
Identify Other-Sabotage in Your Life

Intention: This is a drawing and visualization exercise that helps structure your identity and your support systems. As you draw and mentally process, you may find it helpful to connect your gut, your mental, and your voice consciousnesses.

Materials: Comfortable clothes and uninterrupted time and space to draw. A blank sheet of paper and a writing utensil. (Personally, I love to use colored markers!)

Time: 15–20 minutes

Note: Pre-read the following directions so you can be present in the process as you experience it. This is a helpful exercise to identify your support system outside of judgment and pressures.

Instructions:

Before you begin drawing, interlace your fingers and make a circle with your arms in front of your body. Imagine this to be your sacred white space, a place for you to grow and blossom as a person. This is imperative—all people need a nontoxic area in their lives that allows them the grace and space to become their best selves.

Now, imagine your arms being pushed together from outside the circle. Make the circle smaller and smaller. This is a visual illustration of the outside forces that constrict the space you absolutely need.

Visualize those forces. What's crowding your sacred space and pushing from the outside? These are your other-sabotage items. Sometimes they are noble, necessary, and worth focusing on. At other times they are not. Most of the time, it is very difficult to know or admit what is truly necessary and what can wait or is not your battle in the first place.

As you consider what these other-sabotage items in your life may be and where they come from, draw a large circle in the center of your blank sheet of paper. This represents your sacred white space.

Outside Arrows: Support vs. Sabotage

Draw several arrows that point toward the large circle and several arrows that point away from it. The inward-pointing arrows represent things and people that pressure or sabotage your space. The outward-pointing arrows represent things and people that support your sacred space. Label these arrows with support and sabotage items as they come to mind.

Inside Peace: Leveling Up

On the inside of the circle, consider what is in your control. Write what you are actively doing to claim the sacred space for growth and connect with your Soul Chatter.

This diagram will provide a visual representation of your obstacles and supports when working on your Soul Chatter fluency.

Personal White Space—Other-Sabotage Diagram

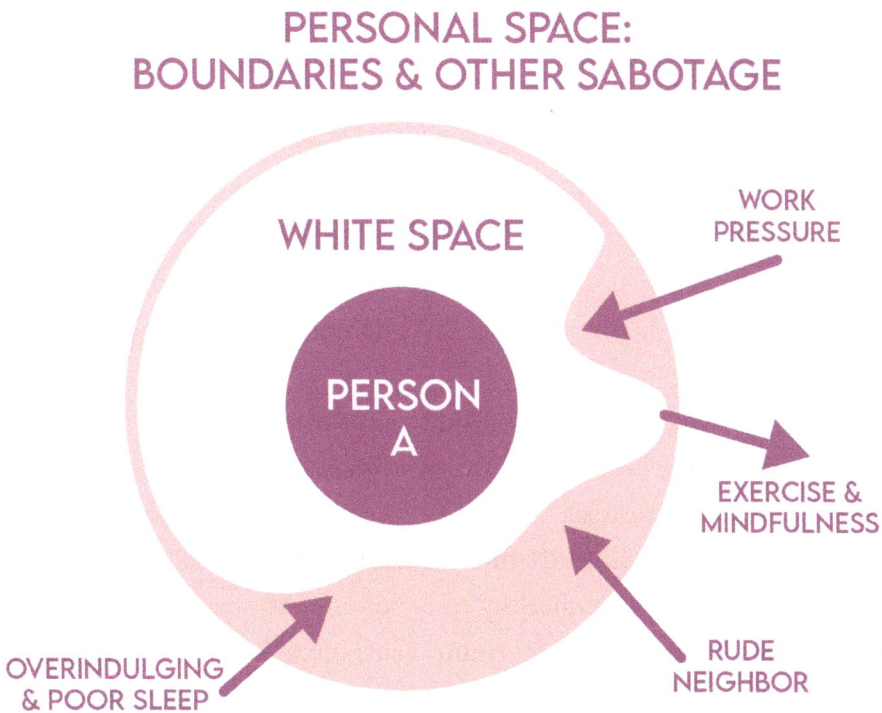

PERSONAL SPACE: BOUNDARIES & OTHER SABOTAGE

WHITE SPACE

PERSON A

WORK PRESSURE

EXERCISE & MINDFULNESS

RUDE NEIGHBOR

OVERINDULGING & POOR SLEEP

All in the Family

The Power of Rules, Roles, and Generational Patterns

Similar to self-sabotage, we may experience roadblocks on our healing journey created by external forces. I will refer to this as *other-sabotage*. Being able to both identify and understand how we might experience other-sabotage is crucial to managing it. Awareness of relationship patterns and how they function is also helpful. Although there are many social systems that have similar dynamics and effects on our life, for our purposes we will focus on the family system.

(Note that similar patterns play out in group environments such as work or other organizations—committees, churches, clubs, and boards, for example.)

Our families and close friends may be of tremendous support during our healing journey, but they may also attempt to sabotage it. (Paradoxically, they may do both at the same time.) The family system is powerful and has hereditary, environmental, and relational influence over us throughout our lives. Although every family operates differently, there are some commonalities in all family systems.

Rules

The rules and patterns of a family are often subtle. They may be difficult to identify, but every family member is aware of the system parameters. In fact, the best way to discover your unique family guidelines may be to ask one of the younger family members about them.

The family rules can be as simple as, "Everyone knows not to wake up Dad before 8:00." Or they may be less overt, such as, "We do not tell anyone that grandfather's death was a suicide."

All families have rules of operation, and most of those rules carry out a necessary function. But when they become secretive or work to the detriment of the individuals, the family rules become toxic.

A healthy family may correct dysfunctional rules they've created as they notice a deficit. But over time, if the unhealthy rules become the norm without being corrected, they may be passed on to future generations and become generational patterns.

Roles

A defining characteristic of all family systems is that its members must fill certain roles, which may become tied to their identities. There is nothing inherently negative about a family role. They can serve a necessary purpose.

One indication of a healthy family system is that functional family roles are somewhat fluid and can be filled by multiple members. Although people typically have a single primary role, they may step into others as needed. For example, when the person who plays the role of the family nurturer is ill or unable to provide that function, another person from the family can step into the caretaker role without destabilizing the family.

One indicator of emotionally unhealthy family systems is they tend to have inflexible roles that members can never break out of. Consequently, these families are less able to adjust to a crisis.

Patterns

Generational patterns are ingrained habits, hereditary tendencies, or regular behaviors that have been handed down from one family member to the next through the family tree. These can look like addiction, abuse, or emotional illness, but they can also be positive qualities, like a propensity for a certain career, a gentle spirit, or a strong work ethic.

Emotional pain and energy, such as shame, guilt, or depression, can be passed down the family line as a generational pattern. But so can emotional healing. The beauty of breaking unhealthy generational patterns is that it benefits not only you but also your descendants. In a very real way, you are giving a gift to your children and your children's children.

The easiest way to identify generational patterns is to make a graph of your family: a genogram. Beside each person's name, write their careers, addictions, emotional issues, and strengths.

Note: Check the supplemental *Sozo Exercise: Genograms* at the end of this chapter if you are interested in looking at the generational patterns of your family.

Understanding Other-Sabotage

The Crabs in the Bucket Effect

A fascinating phenomenon that is taught in family counseling training is the Crabs in the Bucket Effect. Good crabbers know that to prevent their crabs from escaping they should always keep more than one in a bucket. Apparently, when several crabs are in a bucket and one attempts to free itself, the remaining crabs will pull it back into the bucket. Rude.

Similarly, family members will sabotage a relative who is striving to change a personal pattern if they feel the change will have too great an effect on the family. If one member of an emotionally unhealthy family attempts to reject his or her assigned role, the rest of the family will scramble to force the individual back into the previous emotionally unhealthy state—even if it is detrimental to that person.

One psychology professor tells the story of a woman who picked her husband up from rehab with a case of beer in the trunk. The family was not ready for a sober dad. That is an extreme example of a classic crab in the bucket effect. The father was trying to change his role, but the family perceived that change to be threatening to their identity and family functioning. On some level, the wife perceived that a sober husband would alter their family system so greatly that she was unwilling to risk the inevitable changes that his sobriety would bring.

Rules of Other-Sabotage

Other-sabotage is confusing. Why would people push against your efforts? It is especially frustrating and hurtful when it comes from a person you trust or respect. It is often a clash of conflicting agendas that may come from an unexpected source.

Here are five sabotage rules that may be helpful when trying to recognize and manage other-sabotage:

1. We cannot change other people.

2. We cannot allow other people to dictate our value.

3. Generational patterns are not our destiny; we can intentionally choose to keep or change them.

4. We choose our level of *self*.

5. We do not have to accept the role that other people try to assign us.

Other-Sabotage Rule #1: We cannot change other people.

As we begin living from a place of self-love, setting boundaries in our relationships becomes imperative. We embrace the reality that, in all our relationships, we can only be responsible for our side of the equation. In fact, having the courage to honor our own voice and make necessary changes in our own lives—regardless of the support or approval of others—is the best way to start our self-love journey.

Balancing self-love and our love for the people in our lives is an intricate dance and the ultimate goal of every Soul Chatter journey. The intersection of those two missions is where we learn to tango in the tension between enmeshment and differentiation.

Other-Sabotage Rule # 2: We cannot allow other people to dictate our value.

Most emotional pain springs from our desire to feel valued and our need for connection. When we are in a wounded place, we see connection as a way to be validated. We might believe we have value and hope it's true, but we look to others to confirm that truth. As they become our measuring rod, it is easy to perceive our worth through our interpretation of the opinions of others. This dynamic gives the people in our lives, especially our family, a great deal of power.

Let the games begin—the relationship game and the power game. There are a thousand ways to look for validation and a million ways to abuse each other.

To be clear, the power of the family system can also be constructive and our best source of support. Understanding the family rules, roles, and patterns of both our childhood family of origin and our current adult family will aid in developing a framework for understanding our relationship patterns. This gives us the ability to make clear, conscious choices for how we want to respond to our emotional inheritance.

Other-Sabotage Rule # 3: Generational patterns are not our destiny; we can intentionally choose to keep or change them.

During family therapy, I find it helpful to view the family system as a bit of a wild horse that will never fully be broken (and, in all honesty, it shouldn't be). Family systems are strong, powerful, and resilient. Their prime directive is preservation of the system.

All families have rules, roles, and patterns unique to them. The family system does an excellent job of protecting the family at any cost. Too often, however, the protection of the family system might not be what is best for individual members.

Sometimes, the system is not emotionally healthy, and continuing the family as is requires rules to be secretive, roles to be skewed, and unhealthy patterns to be accepted.

An unhealthy family will actually strive to preserve its own unhealthy patterns rather than threaten its current system. The first step of breaking an undesirable family pattern is being aware of its dynamics and the effects on members.

Other-Sabotage Rule # 4: We choose our level of self.

We choose how many of our decisions we will allow others to influence. The realization of other-sabotage in our lives can be especially difficult, as most of us assume the people we care about will support our healing and self-harmonization journey. Yet it confounds us when we realize they don't support us in the way we would like them to.

I have sat with clients who spend a great deal of time and personal energy trying to understand why the people in their lives react the way they do. People are complex, motives are muddled, and often the people we love don't even understand their own selves.

The only outcome we can control is our own decisions. Sometimes the kindest thing we can do for the people we love is to become our best self. They may need to lean on us someday, and we can best support them from a position of strength.

Other-Sabotage Rule # 5: We do not have to accept the role that other people try to assign us.

From birth, we are given a narrative by our family of origin, which unfolds throughout our lives. It serves as a loose script for our response to the pressure and opinions of the people we encounter on our journey. As we mature and develop our own traits and talents, some of the roles we have been assigned may fit, and others may not. Some we grow out of, and others never fit in the first place.

The family system may pressure us to perform some of our expected family roles. Ultimately, it is our choice to fill them or not. Honest conversations identifying our roles and expectations can be a way to connect with the people we care about and is often an avenue to greater personal growth—for us and, many times, for them, too.

Understanding relationship dynamics can be an eye-opener when it comes to our own family. Although we work to respect our relatives, for the sake of our own emotional wellness, it is often good to take a step back and notice energy dynamics and relationship patterns. Calling out unhealthy patterns and other-sabotage may, in the long run, be a positive pivot for many family members.

Roaring Butterflies

In the next chapter, we will proceed to *claiming our power and finding our voice* (Step 5). This empowerment is the natural progression after realizing our worth. When we accept that we are worthy, our message will become important enough to fight for.

Do you remember the butterfly who was too afraid to fly because she had a spot on her wing? Imagine that she claimed her message and accepted her worth. Her first flight over the fields would be glorious. That beautifully spotted butterfly would spread her wings and began to soar.

Sozo Extra Supplemental Healing Exercises
Mini Genogram Exercise

MINI-GENOGRAM FAMILY RELATIONS KEY

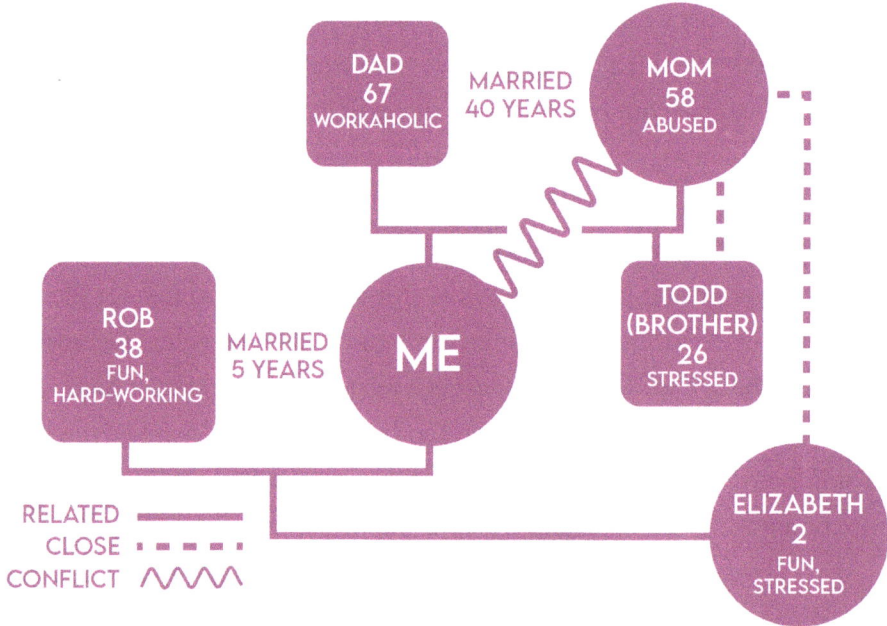

DAD
67
WORKAHOLIC

MARRIED
40 YEARS

MOM
58
ABUSED

ME

ROB
38
FUN,
HARD-WORKING

MARRIED
5 YEARS

TODD
(BROTHER)
26
STRESSED

RELATED ———
CLOSE ▪▪▪▪▪
CONFLICT ∧∧∧∧

ELIZABETH
2
FUN,
STRESSED

Create your own genogram as you look for family dynamic patterns in the space below.

Chapter Six Notes

CHAPTER SEVEN

Step 5: Claim Your Power

Finding Your Voice

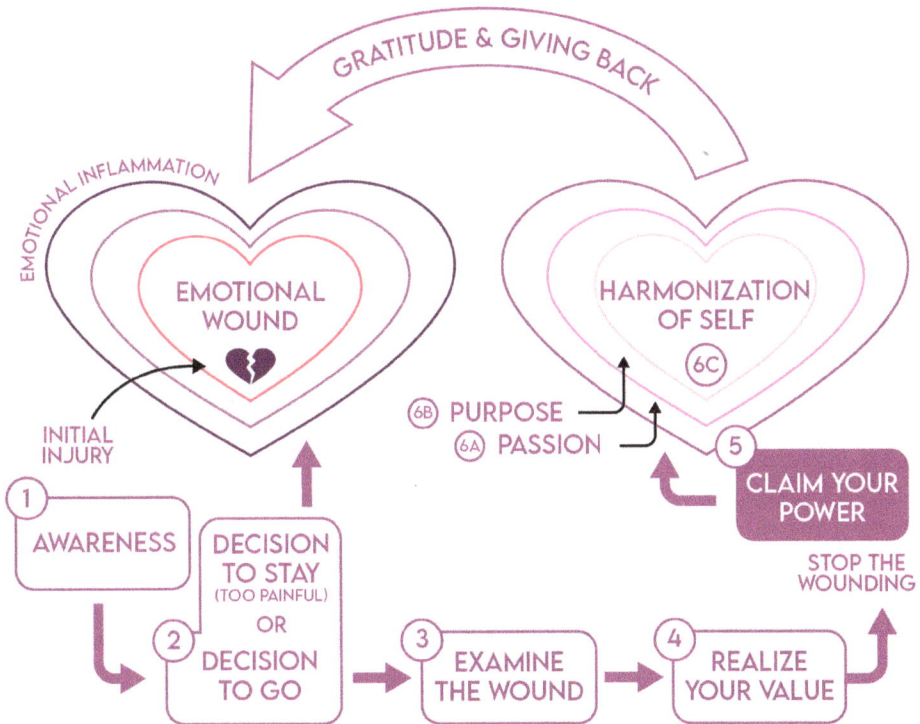

GRATITUDE & GIVING BACK

EMOTIONAL INFLAMMATION

EMOTIONAL WOUND

HARMONIZATION OF SELF
(6C)

INITIAL INJURY

(6B) PURPOSE
(6A) PASSION

1 AWARENESS

DECISION TO STAY (TOO PAINFUL)
OR
2 DECISION TO GO

3 EXAMINE THE WOUND

4 REALIZE YOUR VALUE

5 CLAIM YOUR POWER

STOP THE WOUNDING

Corbett Model of Emotional Healing & Self-Integration™

> Who will let you? That's not the point.
> The point is, who will stop me?[21]
> **—Ayn Rand**

When something inside of you stirs your soul and calls you to action, *you are empowered by passion.*

Claim your power.

You may have been silenced, betrayed, or brought low, yet in the depths of anguish you muster the energy needed to rise from those ashes. You shake your fist and declare, "Not today. I'm not finished yet." *You are empowered to embrace life on your terms.*

Claim your power.

When an injustice is no longer acceptable, your determination sparks the focused thought, "Life is worth fighting for. This is wrong and I will stand for what is right." *You are empowered for a cause.*

Claim your power.

There are few moments in this life more awe-inspiring than when a person wholeheartedly accepts their worth and embraces the passion that bubbles within their being.

Claiming Your Power and Finding Your Voice (Step 5) is the natural progression as you continue your self-harmonization journey. Time on this earth is short, and you have a message to deliver. This is the birth of your authentic self—no apologies, no judgment; just acceptance. Empowerment is born in accepting your worth. Take a deep breath. You are ready.

Empowerment to Courageously Soar

The time for empowering your message is the moment you feel the pull to do so. It's never too late or too soon to find your voice on your quest to energize your passion. You are ready to let go of what has been hindering you and to claim your story on your terms.

You may have felt empowered from a young age. Or you may have lived a full life, raised a family, or retired from a demanding career before feeling the pull. Regardless, you are ready to progress through the healing process and announce your soul song.

With newfound clarity you can progress on your self-harmonization journey and declare, "I'm finally comfortable in my own skin. This is who I am." Bravo—the ideal time to live your life on your terms is when you are ready. This is empowerment.

The aftereffect of embracing your value is that you will no longer be able to accept a life that does not authentically honor your true self. Honoring yourself means living your truth. From that moment on, there will be inevitable changes in your life.

New boundaries will be carved, and relationship patterns will be altered. You can courageously pursue your best self, even if it makes waves. If you feel empowered, *make some waves.* Splash, baby, splash!

A Sozo Healing Story:
Ruby—a Gem of a Gal

Ruby stepped into my office so quietly I almost didn't notice her. She had a stress-worn, gentle face but a furrowed brow. She was soft-spoken yet frazzled as she explained her predicament: "I think I'm experiencing a mini midlife crisis. I'm looking smack-dab at my fiftieth birthday, and I have so many unrealized dreams. Can you just explain to me what happened?"

Later, I asked Ruby how she viewed herself, and she gently replied, "My friends would say I'm kind, a gem of a gal." Then her grin faded into a grimace. Ruby drummed her fingers on the chair as she explained, "I have dedicated my last seventeen years as the administrative manager for one of our area's megachurches. I've embraced my job with unwavering conviction and considered my work to be my honor and my mission."

"There are always people who are in need, and I just do whatever I can to help," Ruby continued. "I've made meals for those who are ill, watched dogs and children when people got in a jam. I've even run errands for staff members, in an effort to make sure the people around me are cared for. My husband and I live in a comfortable enough house. How could I be anything but happy?"

Ruby's voice trailed off, and she gazed at the floor and murmured, "So why am I sitting here talking to you?" In fact, Ruby had come to me for therapy at the suggestion of her boss, the head minister. "I think he may be…concerned that I might be depressed, or angry, or something. I'm not going to kill myself or anything. At least not on purpose."

As Ruby recounted her life story, she did a lot of apologizing. "I asked for a raise several years ago, but the money wasn't really there, so I ought not to have done that. I've always wanted to travel and see the world, but my husband feels more comfortable being at the ranch." She sighed and stifled a sarcastic eye roll.

"Our kids don't live at home anymore, but they have had a lot of needs that require most of our extra cash. Then there's Mom," Ruby sighed again. "She's getting up there in years and needs a little extra help. I have two brothers, who live closer to her than I do, but they find it difficult to see her so fragile, and it just makes sense for me to run up there and help our mother out. I have been busy trying to love the people in my life and being the person everyone needs me to be for so long. I may have forgotten who I set out to be."

"Ruby, you have done a lot of deep from-the-core sighing," I observed. "Do you think your inner voice may be trying to say something? Take a deep energizing breath. Right at this moment. What do you need to say?"

"My first thought is nothing. So much nothing I can't get past it." Ruby caught herself sighing again. "Then all my thoughts rush together at once. I guess I'm numb."

Ruby took another intentional breath. "When I think about it, I wonder why my needs are not important. Why does no one care for and take care of me the way I care for and take care of them? I have been coddling the people in my life for years, and I am now realizing that I need to value myself or no one ever will."

"Ruby, you have lost your voice. But you can still reclaim it if you choose to," I encouraged.

As was her way, Ruby glanced at her feet and fidgeted in her shoes. The silence of thoughts filled the air. After a time, I heard Ruby quietly but confidently speak, "Why, yes. I would like to get my voice back."

The weeks that followed proved a powerful period for Ruby. She was determined to reconnect with her core self, and as we worked through a few helpful exercises, I observed as she experienced some powerful epiphanies.

One afternoon, Ruby came into my office ready to participate in a Sozo exercise called *The Green Goo Experience*. It turned out to be a bit of a revelation for her. I explained the procedure: "For the exercise today, we are going to sit over this tarp, and I am going to pass you small baggies of green goo. I would like you to imagine that each baggie is full of disgusting, maggot-infested, toxic green gunk." Ruby looked tentative (and a bit creeped out), but she chuckled as she sat down.

"Are you ready, Ruby?"

"As ready as I'll ever be," she giggled nervously.

We sat down and started the Green Goo Experience. I began by handing Ruby her first baggie of green goo.

"Here is some toxic green goo. Could you hold this for me, please?" I asked.

"Sure, I... guess," Ruby replied.

One by one, I continued to give Ruby another baggie, and another, until finally she looked uncomfortable and a bit irritated.

"Wait. What do you want me to do with all of this disgusting green goo?" Ruby wondered aloud.

"I don't know. It's up to you," I replied. "What *are* you going to do with it?"

"I'd like to give it back. Can I?"

"No. But why don't you ask me if *I* would like any?"

"Okay. Do *you* want to take some of this green goo back?"

"No, thank you," I replied gently but firmly. "I don't want the green goo."

"Wait!" Ruby bristled. "You did not tell me that part. What do you mean by *no, thank you*? You can't say that."

"Of course, I can, and so can *you*. Let's try this again. Ruby, here is another bag of green goo. Could you take this for me?"

"No, thank you. I don't want that crap. Is it really that easy?"

"Yes, Ruby," I chuckled. "It takes some practice, but yes, it really is that easy."

Once we get used to the idea that we don't have to make other people happy at our own expense—and that we can say no when people ask us to do something we don't want to do—it *is* actually that easy. It is okay to say *no*.

We must give ourselves permission to speak our minds and let our voices express how we feel, instead of carrying burdens or frustrations that are not ours. We always have the option to decline when other people try to pass us their toxic emotional burdens and extend their inner chaos into our lives. In fact, not only is that all right, but it is often the only emotionally healthy choice.

In this Sozo experiential exercise, the green goo represents the toxic energy and muck that is ever present in our world. It's like *weltschmerz*, an old German expression that roughly translates to "world pain." Each time someone dumps on us (and we let them), we take on their emotionally toxic energy. Over time, we become burdened and bogged down with an accumulation of other people's frustrations and pain.

Ruby gathered techniques to keep her emotional runway clear. She began to recognize other-sabotage, identifying who and what was intruding on her personal circle. She learned to set boundaries and notice the red flags when she was falling back into unhealthy relationship patterns. I was honored to accompany Ruby on her journey to optimal emotional wellness. As she grew determined and intentional, Ruby realized that she had the right to ask for what she needed and practiced the ability to politely assert herself without feeling guilty.

Later that summer, Ruby bounded into my office, excited to tell me about her Monday morning coup d'état. "I found my voice," Ruby cheered! "For the last four months, my church has been undergoing a renovation. At the end of each day, the construction foreman has been marching into my office, spewing and cursing and taking out his frustrations on my equipment. Last Friday, he came barreling in and slammed his fist on my newly repaired copy machine. In that instant, I decided I would not allow him to bring his disrespect into my work environment. I politely asked him where his truck was parked. He said, 'In the bottom parking lot. Why?' "

"So, I said to him, 'Your tools are in your truck. You won't mind if I go use them?' He looked confused," Ruby recounted. " 'You see, the machines in this office are my responsibility, just like the tools in your truck are for you.' I clearly explained, 'When you come into this office and disrespect my equipment, it would be the same as if I went to your truck and helped myself to the use of your tools.' "

Ruby held her head up and her shoulders back as she told her tale. Then she hesitated and burst into a full belly laugh. "I have never seen a grown man's eyes get so big. He froze and replied, 'No ma'am. I will ask next time.' Then he slowly backed out the door, pivoted, and walked briskly to his truck. From that moment on, we've had a great understanding."

Ruby had found her voice and learned to express her needs in a clear and direct way, not just to her coworkers but also to her husband and children. As she experienced inner peace and satisfaction, she learned how to be assertive and eventually found the grace not to be passive-aggressive.

During our last visit Ruby was thrilled to share that she had requested (and received) a well-deserved raise from her boss, and she excitedly mentioned that her husband was taking her to Aruba for an anniversary trip. She felt very optimistic about her life and was excited for her future. As she stood up to leave, she glanced out the window and smiled, "Living your authentic truth is powerful. You don't have to be loud to roar."

Using the Power of Empowerment

We have all sat on the edge of our cushy theater seat during that nail-biting scene when the reluctant hero walks away from the challenge before her. Just as your heart sinks, she pauses and gets that look in her eye (you know the one). With a flash of unbridled energy, she leans into her authentic self and courageously saves the day. We cry, we cheer, we can finally breathe again. This is the power of empowerment. You have that.

Each of us has the ability to connect to the depth of our being and access the power of our authentic self. Existing in this world as fully *you* is wholehearted living. It is the unfolding of the human condition. We all have access to the raw and real power of authenticity, yet we often fear to connect with it.

Empowerment is knowing our gifts and having the courage to be vulnerable enough to share them. Conforming and putting up walls to avoid emotional exposure requires so much of our energy that we eventually become depressed, hopeless, and exhausted. Empowerment is taking the energy we have been using to maintain personas and emotional walls and refocusing it to enliven our authenticity and becoming. The power of that unique inner beauty opens doors and changes lives.

The Art of Being Assertive While Not Being Aggressive

Being respectfully other-centered while valuing our own needs can be a precarious balance. As people claim their empowerment and find their voices, they may feel awkward using them. The result is that they become stressed and aggressive while trying to make their point. This can be the case for people who are not in the habit of using their voice. Honestly expressing our message without becoming aggressive is an art form that may require some intentional practice.

Understanding your worth and knowing that your message is a vital piece of the tapestry of life may help you calmly state what needs to be said or do what needs to be done. You can hone the art of being assertive by giving yourself permission to communicate your feelings respectfully and clearly and by allowing others to do the same.

Firmly and authentically clarifying your needs is an important habit in all healthy relationships. In order to maintain positive dynamics in your relationships, it is important to understand that assertiveness and aggressiveness are completely different interactions. Being conscious of aggressive (toxic) and assertive relationship dynamics can help you balance or even avoid situations in which there is no possibility of a positive outcome.

Aggressiveness

Aggressiveness is a dynamic that is best to avoid in healthy, long-term relationships. Ironically, relationship aggression often arises as an overactive, frustrated response when assertiveness has not been practiced. Being aggressive is primarily an abuse of power or a fear response.

Wild animals are aggressive. Athletes and abusers use aggression to intimidate their opponents. Traditional childhood gender rules may come into play—boys are allowed to be aggressive and girls are expected to be compliant. Mixed messages from our environment and lack of support for dealing with our frustrations may lead to passive-aggressive behavior.

In our effort to maintain healthy relationships, we can practice being fair and assertive. It is the art of calling out wrongs in a calm and honest way without assigning blame, guilt, or shame.

Passive-Aggressiveness

We give away our power for a number of reasons—for example, not wanting to appear mean, not being comfortable with assertiveness, or feeling powerless. We allow people to say things to us that are hurtful or offensive, and we pretend to brush them off.

Years of feeling unappreciated and letting other people set our agenda allows for a frustrated, powerless, and deeply bitter human. Our energy is sapped, and we begin to give up our passions and purpose, resigning ourselves to lives we may not have chosen.

In our frustration, we may interpret others' efforts at communication as especially harsh and seek revenge in our defense. Passive-aggressive communication often comes from people who feel they are backed in a corner and do not have choices. After a long period of unstated needs, they overreact out of frustration or become unexpectedly aggressive. They may also do aggressive things in secret. Passive-aggressive behavior never produces a healthy relationship dynamic.

Assertiveness

Assertive living does not bottle up feelings, eat them, or push them down. Emotions are experienced and acknowledged in an appropriate way and in a timely manner. It is not necessary to manipulate other people but, instead, to express ideas and directions truthfully and directly.

Assertiveness is a healthy relationship dynamic in which we state our needs and remain respectful of other people's feelings and rights. Assertive individuals are confident and friendly and value both themselves and the people around them.

When you live an assertive life, you instinctively realize that you have value (Step 4) and you respect your relationships. You appreciate thoughts and feelings, recognizing that they must be heard and processed. Relationship boundaries are expressed, recognized, and enforced, because saying no to the things you do not want to do provides balance so you can say a wholehearted *yes* to the things that bring you joy.

Taking Your Show on the Road

In the next section, we will highlight the *Soul Soaring* leg of our self-harmonization journey, giving voice to our inner children. This process will energize our passion (Step 6a) and propel us on to consider our purpose (Step 6b).

Persevere—you are so close! This is the time to spread your wings and soar through the silver linings of those formerly dark clouds.

Sozo Supplemental Exercise:
The Green Goo Experience

For those passionate chefs who would like to enjoy their own green goo experience, here is the recipe.

Green Goo Recipe

In a large bowl, mix together:

- 1 cup flour

- 1 cup cornmeal

- 8 drops of green food coloring. Add a few drops of brown if you'd like. (Play with a few colors to get it putrid looking.)

- 1 ½ cups water

- Optional: Add ½ cup coffee grounds

Knead the dough, adding more water until gooey. Put handful-size dollops in small ziplock bags.

Chapter Seven Notes

SECTION THREE: SOUL SOARING

*Soaring Thirty-Thousand Feet
Over a Parched World*

Visionary Living

Section Three Letter from Virginia

Dear Soul-journer,

Soul Soaring is an evolved stage in our self-harmonization journey. In Section 3 of our Soul Chatter journey guide, our destination is the contented state of authentic living. As we learn to navigate the headwinds and turbulence of Soul Soaring, we will enhance our flight with hands-on techniques designed to embrace our passion and realize our purpose. We will maneuver through Step 6 and 7 of the Corbett Model for Emotional Healing and Self-Harmonization™.

During this leg of the Soul Chatter journey, we experience flight, our inner wisdom becoming our rudder. From this vantage point, we can access our wound-wisdom. It is common to feel an overwhelming sense of gratitude.

We may feel compelled to embrace those fellow travelers who are in an emotionally painful place on their own journey. Their pain resonates with us because we have been where they are. *Healed people heal people.* Restoration comes full circle. Our emotional wound begins to scar over as it finds a purpose.

Declare yourself free to soar and refuse to allow the pull of gravity to keep you tethered to this earth. This is your time; your passion calls. I am excited for you and the life to follow. Big encouraging hugs!

Stay well,

Virginia

Section Three Preface

Soul Soaring.

In the peace of the morning, I watched the sun rise. A damp breeze snuck through my slightly open window, accompanied by songs of morning birds. At the top edge of my window glided a majestic hawk, sweeping across the sky like she owned it. "Well, hello there. You are magnificent. How did you know I was completing the section on Soul Soaring?"

I smiled at the God-wink, caught in the graceful *awe* of her flight. Floating above the trees, she was effortless. Her outstretched wings confidently held as they surfed the waves of the wind and found their way over the horizon. Then, just as she began to disappear from my view, she turned around abruptly and headed toward me. As she made her flyby, my soul soared with hers.

This is soul soaring—effortlessly riding the wind, as we do what we were built to do, occasionally allowing necessary space for the comfortable and always having unconditional grace for the afflicted. While soul soaring, we draw on our courage to chase our passions and the steadfastness to accept our purpose. We are buoyed by our reverence for life and our gratitude for living.

You are here. Appreciate your journey. Give yourself a bear hug, and allow the tingle to travel down your spine, all the way to your toes. This is your adventure. Enjoy the lift of soul-soaring freedom and the call of the destination that awaits.

CHAPTER EIGHT

Step 6a: Discover and Embrace Your Passion

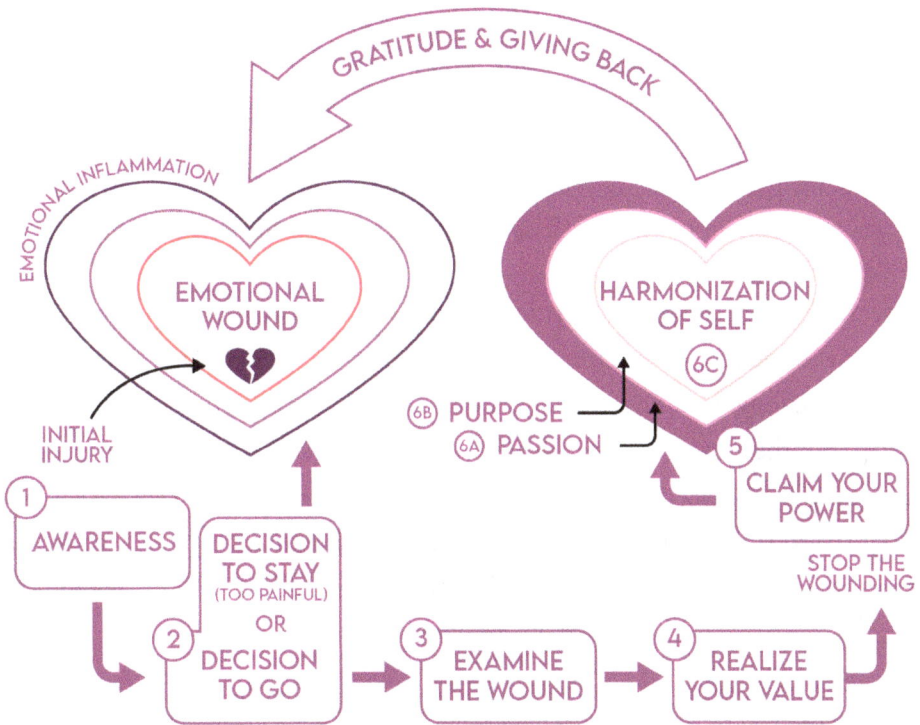

Corbett Model of Emotional Healing & Self-Integration™

To live is the rarest thing in the world.

Most people exist, that is all.[22]

—Oscar Wilde

Confession: I am a sucker for passion—mine, yours, anyone's really. I have found that I can absorb the energy of a passionate person. Being around them always invigorates my life. *Passion is infectious.*

I've witnessed a spark of life when the embers of hope were smoldering. *Passion is invigorating.*

Leaning into passion can energize our state of being. All things being equal, the most passionate person will always lead the pack. *Passion is powerful.*

Wisdom-Breathed Passion

Living a passion-fueled life is a bold and daring art form that is unique to our being and vital to our self-harmonization journey. Passion dims if not energized and expires if continually denied. Conversely, passion breathes life when authentically engaged and expands into dare-to-imagine possibilities.

Embracing passion (Step 6a) provides fuel for our Soul Chatter trek. It enables our inspiration to work in tandem with our logic and ignores the obstacles that may block our pursuits.

The dilemma of seeking authentic passion is that it is difficult to define since it is unique to each person. Over time, we may have allowed the world to distract or numb us until we no longer feel the self-connection necessary to follow our own hearts. Not only that, but the cacophony of judgment and opinions relentlessly pulls us away and demands our focus, essentially pouring sand on our fire.

We have roles to fill and obligations to meet. Sometimes those demands and expectations are self-imposed, but too often they are transplants from someone else's dream.

Pressing On

Courageous passion is not a thinking endeavor but a rich journey. It meanders and forms over time, eventually leading us to a place of fulfilling our purpose (Step 6b). Engaging our passion converts personal energy into realized dreams and renders a unique outcome that is beyond our direct control.

As we became empowered (Step 5), we learned to hush the noise of the world. In that peace we can hear the whispers of our Soul Chatter and be assured it will always point the way.

A Sozo Passion Story:
The Artful Life of Passion

Years ago, when I first met Dianna, she had black hair with a streak of white. Now, several decades later she has white hair with streaks of black. Trust me, her flair fills the room and her zeal is contagious. Recently, I was able to attend one of Dianna's "Bodacious Blooms" art workshops. Being with her in her element added a new dimension to her persona and helped me appreciate the intricate layers of love and life produced by her passionate living.

Her class met in a large room perched above a trendy gallery, which provided the perfect backdrop for the weekend art retreat. The aroma of obstinately strong coffee strengthened the resolve of the art students as they filtered into the room. I watched as the budding artists placed their canvases on easels and began fidgeting with their brushes.

The promise of white space provided a hopeful atmosphere, and Dianna smiled knowingly. She began encouraging her students with possibilities of what they were about to create. Their connection to their art, I noticed, became the medium that gave them permission to battle their fears and release any obstacles that might have threatened their creative flow.

Every layer of paint energized transformations of both art and heart. Laughter alternated with stillness. The occasional expletive intertwined with "Damn, I guess I just needed to get out of my head." Or "Wow, I didn't know I could do this!" As the day unfolded, it became apparent that finding our voice doesn't always require words.

After the workshop, I had a chance to decompress with Dianna and process the dynamics I had witnessed. Naturally, she was already aware of them. "I was awed at how your students claimed their power and experienced their voice," I noted. "Confidence and self-expression transcended the canvas. I believe there was a lot of emotional healing that took place today, not to mention some fabulous art."

She smiled and said, "It's fun to hear you say that. There's always something magical that happens for people in the process of pushing their creative boundaries."

I nodded, and the therapist in me couldn't resist diving deeper into Dianna's story. "You must feel a sense of contentment as you paint and teach," I said to her. "It's so natural for you. I know you've been creating for decades. What is the spark of passion that keeps you going back to your studio, painting after painting?"

"Hmmm." Dianna took a deep breath, glanced at the ceiling, and worked her way through her mental Rolodex of students and her years of being a creative. With a sigh she concluded, "Passion."

"I've discovered a few things about passion," she continued. "The way you find it is to follow the things that delight your heart. I don't care what you do as long as it has a spark for you. It can be very simple. Maybe recycling gives you that joy. Then start recycling. When you do, you will find one door open and then the next. It will guide you, and you will find your purpose."

"What an adventure!" I commented.

"Absolutely!" She smiled. "It's definitely been a journey. My bliss has always flirted with the arts. It began with music—clarinet, piano, guitar, and singing through college. Although that was truly more of my mother's passion *for* me, I felt somewhat competent and interested.

"Growing up, I felt I didn't have a voice or that my voice was wrong. It wasn't until I discovered photography—and the magic of the darkroom—that I truly claimed my voice and began to express it. Although there were twists and turns, I embraced painting, not just as my passion but as a way of life. It's like air—without it, I suffocate."

I understood exactly what she was describing. I asked, "Have there been times you felt suffocated?" Dianna glanced down and began sinking into her thoughts. "There have been a few turning points that bumped me back on track."

She continued, "I remember feeling *off* after giving birth to my second daughter. (Postpartum depression was barely a word then.) I chose to fight back and get intensive therapy—and yes, it was intense. After several months, my therapist asked me what brings me joy. That was a painful question in that moment, and I sputtered through the usual list: what I had to do that day, my husband, and my kids. She gave me *the* look. That was not what she meant, and to tell you the truth, I didn't have a clue how to honestly answer. So, I did the next best thing. I gave her a long blank stare.

"On another occasion, I found myself in an office job that carried expectations of perfectionism and didn't allow me time to paint. That double whammy drained my life blood and put me in a virtual straitjacket. Looking back, I realize I'm a creative. Boxing me in with perfectionism is toxic. Lacking oxygen is a good way to describe that time in my life. I felt totally defeated, insignificant, and, quite frankly, my creative spirit was withering away.

"I now see that I had begun to believe the lie that I was 'less than' and inconsequential. Once that dark thought takes hold of you, it's difficult to shake. I'm grateful that, somewhere in the midst of feeling suffocated, there was a turning point. I was able to spread paint on a canvas again. It was not until I fully stepped back into my bliss that I internalized the effect that experience had been having on my well-being."

The room was muted by twilight as we both felt the peace of contentment. Finally, I pushed on and asked Dianna what she now knew from her current vantage point.

"*Passion is our compass*. I now view the entire world through that lens. My friends always chuckle when we're on walks because I'm constantly stopping to observe the way the light is hitting a surface, the shape of a flower, the pattern of a crack in the sidewalk, the movement of a beetle.

"I'm mesmerized as I absorb the play of shape, patterns, and the interaction of color and movement. It fuels my soul and continuously inspires and influences my work.

"*Sometimes the biggest obstacle to my work is me*. I am learning to get out of my own way. There are times when I still push things forward in an effort to control a painting (also in life!). It's only when I stop and let go, allowing God to create through me, that I feel serene, confident, and energized. Who else is better to help me create than the ultimate creator?!

"*I do not have to frantically chase my passion*. It's part of me and has its own seasonality. My passion for art has become a consuming lifestyle. My life needs art. I read about it, dream about it, collect it, and sometimes obsess over it. Without it I get cranky, unnerved, and disheartened.

"Ironically, at the same time, I am actually not driven to do it. I typically don't paint when I don't *feel* it. I work on the business and marketing of my art instead. It has its own flow and will pull me back. I know I will return to painting when I have the overwhelming urge to go create. Many things do drag me away, and at those times I remind myself that it is temporary and is happening for a reason."

"Thank you for sharing that." I soaked it all in. "Your journey is awe-inspiring. I have several coaching clients who are able to let go and be a conduit for creativity. That is one of the surprising joys on the path to self-harmonization. Do you feel your purpose is realized in the process of embracing your passion?"

"Absolutely! My singular intention is to share joy," Dianna beamed. "I feel blessed to connect with a community that loves art as much as I do, and it is thrilling to use my vibrant art and workshops to help others become more comfortable and confident in their creative voices. That is my joy and my way of being grateful as I give back."

Universal Passion Rules

Three Truths about Passion

Intentionally pursuing your passion is much like a high-stakes treasure hunt in the desert using an old worn-out map for a guide. The quest is full of twists, turns, and bursts of eureka-excitement. At times, abrupt halts leave you wondering why you started the trek in the first place.

Life is an adventure, and you are unveiling the richness of your authentic story. Here are a few passion truths that may prove helpful as you navigate your journey.

Passion Truth #1: Authentic passion energizes.

Authentic passion is invigorating and restorative. There is a visible change when a person engages their passion—their eyes light up, their mind becomes more alert, and their mood elevates. So, enjoy the process of engaging your passion. Follow what uniquely stirs your soul. Allow it to develop, and determine to commit the resources for mastery.

Passion Truth #2: Passion trumps fear—if you let it.

Passion and fear are the fuel and the brakes used to navigate our Soul Chatter journey. Passion propels us forward, whereas fear decelerates our momentum. Facing down our fear requires a certain amount of faith in the process as we learn to trust our inner wisdom. Boldness may be required to break through any barriers that deplete our energy.

The battle between passion and fear has a meeting place in every human heart. Don't let anyone steal your joy. The best interpreter of what emanates from your soul is *you*.

Passion Truth #3: Passion is a journey that is uncovered by its earnest pursuit.

As you engage, your passion-quest will take on a life of its own. As you courageously pursue your passion, you will convert curiosity to mastery. Ideas will become reality. Be expectant. Perhaps the destination of your passion seems hazy now, but don't be afraid to dream big as you allow for possibilities. The unfolding of your passion and the relevance of its message will land exactly where it should.

While pursuing your passion, you will likely become weary and occasionally discouraged at times. But with the perseverance of passion:

- You feel inspired and energized.

- You gain confidence.

- Needed resources become available.

- Unexpected opportunities and connections arise.

- Your story becomes punctuated with vibrancy and unexpected joy.

Remembering What Sparks Joy
Awakening Passion

During the pursuit of passion, many people feel a softening within them as they reconnect with the vulnerability necessary to unveil their authentic self. In many ways the journey to become comfortable in our own skin is a return to truths we knew as children.

Our child-selves were more accepting and had intimate relationships with things that have been tucked away over the years. Harmonization of our authentic selves is the process that respects each of our inner children and empowers them to have a voice in our holistic being.

American poet E.E. Cummings understood the courage and determination of the self-harmonization journey:[23]

> To be nobody but yourself in a world which is doing its best day and night to make you like everybody else means to fight the hardest battle which any human being can fight and never stop fighting. ... It takes courage to grow up and become who you really are.

The battle to authentically follow our passions despite the risks will not always be appreciated by the world. For many people, seeing real authenticity may be a harsh reminder that they are not being true to their own selves. But we are too far along on our journey for outside pressures to deter us now.

Be aware that those who dare to be different may be ostracized, revered, or both. That is the potential risk for anyone who has ever authentically pursued their passions. Despite the obstacles, honoring our passions ultimately allows us to authentically live our lives on our terms.

Self-Care for Our Inner Children

Perhaps the ultimate self-care is accepting and nurturing our inner children, allowing them to have a voice and mature. We can acknowledge the desires and dreams of each of our parts as we understand who we are and what vitalizes us. Self-exploration can help us identify our earnest desires and recognize that some of our self-sabotage and impulsive patterns stem from the protectiveness of our inner children.

The following exercise is designed to help you reconnect to your inner children by considering early memories that may be fundamental to your identity. This process reframes and energizes your sense of self.

A Sozo Art Journal Exercise:
A Walk Down Memory Lane

This is a contemplative art journal exercise to reconnect and give voice to your inner children. Take your time. Don't rush through your memories. Like butterflies, they tend to have a seat on your shoulder only when you are still.

<u>Materials</u>: A journal without lines, your medium of choice (i.e., colored pencils, markers, crayons, or watercolors), your favorite beverage, a box of tissues, and a quiet, uninterrupted space.

Part 1

Get comfortable and find your calm. Smile. Take a deep breath and arrange your art supplies. Anchor yourself to the present by using your senses:

Taste your beverage as you sip from your glass.

Listen to your favorite music or enjoy silence as you become aware of your sense of hearing.

Feel your body and acknowledge sensory messages as you breathe deeply.

Allow a moment to let your being adjust to and be enveloped by your surroundings. Take a deep cleansing breath. Can you sense your heart beating? Breathe in again through your nose, filling your lungs with air. Pause. Let your breath flow out of your mouth completely.

This is a unique moment in time. Determine to savor it. When you are ready, close your eyes and picture a memory. Think back to a time when you were very young. We are not searching for a positive or negative memory, just one that anchors you as a small child. Let the moments pass, but do not try to control or process it. Just allow yourself to be present in an early memory.

When you feel ready, open your eyes and begin drawing your memory. Don't critique or judge your work. Move your pen as you capture this moment. There are no rules. This is your memory, and you can connect with it however you choose to, or not at all. You can draw colors or patterns, just so long as they tap into that memory. Draw until you feel complete.

As you draw, ask yourself:

- What was I doing in the memory?

- Who were the participants?

- What was I feeling at that time?

- What was important to me?

When you've finished, pick up the page and look at what you've drawn. Take your time to study the image. Then ask yourself the following questions:

- What is the first feeling I have when looking at this drawing?

- Am I independent or dependent on something or someone?

- How does revisiting this moment make me react?

- How do I view myself?

- How do I think people view me in this memory?

- How does this moment speak to me?

- What would I like to say to the child in this memory?

Why do you think you chose to capture this particular moment? There have been thousands upon thousands of moments in your life. Why did you zero in on this one?

Often, we tend to frame our memories in ways that support our perception of ourselves and what we believe to be our place in the world. Our memories support our identity. For example, one woman I worked with saw herself as a victim, and when prompted, she recalled many early memories that reinforced that perceived identity. So, ask yourself:

- What do I like about the image of myself?

- Is there something I don't like?

- What does it mean to see myself in this way?

- How does this memory connect to my life now?

- Do I have a specific view of life? What is my role in it?

Note: The second part of this exercise can be done immediately if you feel ready to move forward. However, if you need time to process and rest, don't hesitate to connect and respond to your own needs.

Part 2

Repeat the drawing exercise, this time making an effort to emphasize a positive image of yourself. Redraw your memory using this positive perspective to support the child in the picture. If your original drawing was already what you wished it to be, draw another memory.

This time your goal is to reinforce a positive view of yourself by drawing a moment when you felt empowered. Think of a memory that reinforces and aligns with that image.

Example: In the first drawing, I am observing the outdoors and enjoying the presence of my dog and family, but passively so. In my revised drawing, I would like to depict myself as being creative and actively connected rather than simply standing by and observing.

When you finish, pick up the drawing and study it. Ask yourself the following questions:

- What feelings do I have when I see this memory?

- What is my first thought?

- How do I view myself in this drawing?

- Is it different than how I feel about myself now?

- What does this picture say about me?

Art can tap into our experiences and wrangle feelings that words cannot capture. If this is a tool that you enjoy, you can expand your art journaling portfolio. Deep emotional healing draws from a place in our being that needs no words.

Making Sense of the Pieces of Me

The complexities of the human psyche beautifully baffle even the most learned researchers. Its orchestration of memories and emotions harnesses our innate need for safety and connection to override all other systems.

Our own being keeps us safe by granting access to only the parts of memories that can be processed at the current time. Isn't this brilliant? Isn't this frustrating? Isn't this confounding? Yes, to all the above!

There are many nuances of this process, but three are particularly helpful to keep in mind for our purposes:

- As our psyche releases memories in parts, there may be large and important elements of our experience that we struggle to recall. It is common for a person receiving therapy to recover details of events as they feel more and more safe throughout the healing process.

- When we experience a memory—especially a difficult one—it will likely be a sensory memory and may not be logical. We might remember a smell, a sound, or how we felt at that time.

- Unprocessed memories from our childhood are often embedded with the emotions we felt at the time, and our perspective on those memories is limited to the age we were when we experienced them. Unprocessed memories are kept in our psyche's storage vault when they occurred, without being updated. They may be pure in a childlike way but can be missing the insights of an adult.

Our psyche's elaborate dance to protect our being from dark and toxic realities is beautiful. We can appreciate what has been done within our being to keep us safe. But at some point, we are ready to accept our reality and live into the fullness of our harmonized being.

Soul Chatter fluency allows us to holistically accept who we are and access the wisdom of our being—to move beyond the sensory memories and access our passion to live out our purpose.

The Dance

Passion to Purpose

For some people, the details of their passion seem clear, but for others, the specifics are clarified by passion's pursuit. Our passion trek energizes us and helps complete our story. Even the wildest successes feel empty when they are void of passion.

The passion that vitalizes us doesn't have to be public; it doesn't have to be our career or a source of income. It can be something exclusive to us. Society tends to pervert the concept of passion. Give yourself permission to follow your passion for passion's sake. It's not for anyone (even you) to judge.

What flows through you and is delivered as a product of your passion connects to a need you might not understand or even realize exists. Beware of overthinking passion. It is a soul language not easily translated into words.

To illustrate this concept, try succinctly describing the greatest love you have ever felt. History's greatest writers and poets have devoted lifetimes attempting to put strong feelings of love into words—and they are still working on it. Words are rarely adequate to convey strong feelings or states of being. Passion is a means to translate the indescribable into something tangible.

The Next Step: Purpose

In Step 6a, we explored our passion and its pursuit. Passion is the fuel for our journey as we engage our muse and lean into our personal genius. Our passion-quest's outcome may be the message that leaves our unique imprint on this world and outlasts our earthly existence.

On the next step of our journey to self-harmonization, we will explore the intricacies of the elaborate dance of purpose (Step 6b). Although it is possible to live a full life without ever clearly identifying our purpose, the pursuit of our passion tends to illuminate our understanding of it.

Chapter Eight Notes

Step 6b: Find and Follow Your Purpose

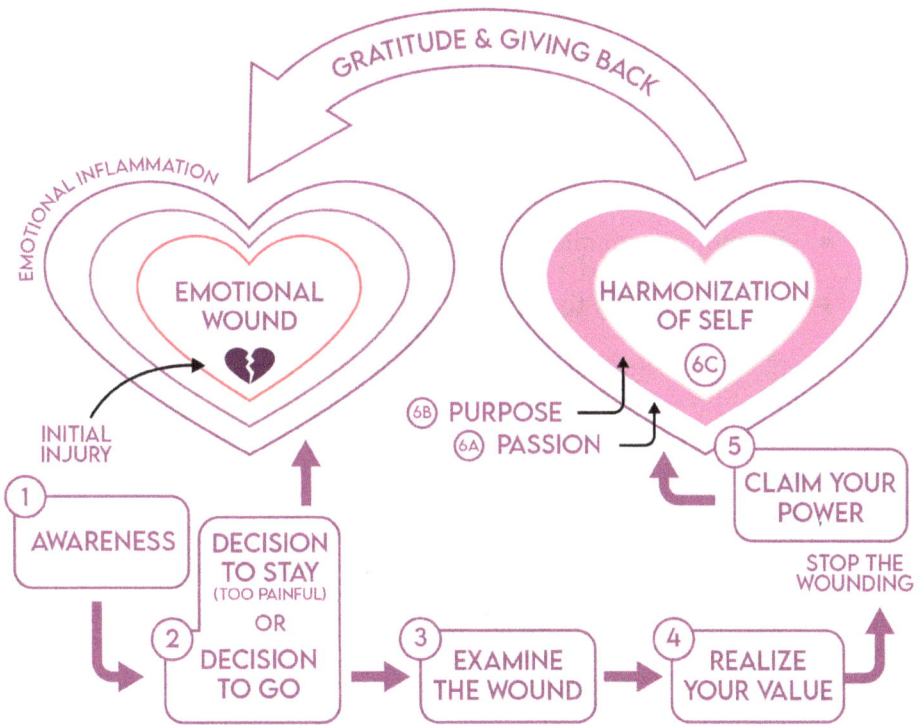

Corbett Model of Emotional Healing & Self-Integration™

> We can make the best or the worst of it. I hope you make the best of it. And I hope you see things that startle you. I hope you feel things you never felt before. I hope you meet people with a different point of view. I hope you live a life you're proud of. If you find that you're not, I hope you have the strength to start all over again.[24]
> **—Eric Roth**

Boom! If you could, this very moment, transport yourself back to the last experience that took your breath away, where would you go? There are specks of time that leave us utterly amazed. As you lean into that memory, relive it. What was your awe-muse? Was it:

- the most panoramic sunset ever?

- a newborn's tiny fingers?

- the unexpected colors in the eyes of someone you deeply love?

Those micro-encounters are *awe*-moments. Awe is a Soul Chatter experience. When we come face-to-face with awe, we use our bodily senses to absorb it into our being. In that moment, what we are witnessing is not intellectually definable. Our thinking center stalls as it struggles to comprehend. It malfunctions, unable to categorize concepts into files it cannot readily access.

Just like a spinning wheel on our computer screen, our mind center freezes, and we are rendered speechless. In response, our being center takes over, bypassing our thinking center (which has proved inadequate during this operation), and relies on our senses to interpret. The noise that involuntarily escapes our mouth as we stand stunned in slack-jawed wonderment is, indeed, "Ahhh." This is *awe*.

We humans have an innate need for awe-infused moments, when we connect with our being and experience a knowing that transcends our intellect. Encounters with awe rev our passion and point us in the direction of our purpose. During awe-experiences, we are momentarily forced to live in the reality of the present. Our thinking center—including all the chatter that resides there—is silenced, and our being experiences the peace and calm of fully living in the now.

Awe instantly confirms what our soul already knows: we are a vital part of something greater. This Soul Chatter connection can be a eureka moment, providing a stepping stone to present-moment living. It invites us to energize our passion and, ultimately, lean into our purpose.

The Tapestry of Purpose

It may be helpful to imagine the enactment of our purpose as an intricate tapestry we can only see from the back side. When we view the mission that entwines our purpose, it appears as messy snares of colorful threads and knots. From our vantage point, the tapestry of life looks confusing and senseless.

Perhaps our mission is to move a blue thread from left to right, though doing so may seem to make little sense. But there is a bigger picture. If we could change our perspective to the front side, we would see the beautiful tapestry being weaved. We would find that the blue thread we contributed through our passion is vital to an awe-infused design.

Consider that the mark we make on this world may be the product of our passion. As we trust and allow our gifts and talent to be guided by our passion, we may unknowingly fulfill our purpose.

The Healing Power of Connecting with Awe

Our personal and collective *awe*-experiences can be a source of healing. On a personal level, awe can be a finger-snap, crisply calling us to return to a state of present-moment being. This reminds us to quit our obsessive thinking, slow down and enjoy the majesty that envelopes us.

Our awe-encounters soothe our thinking center—where stress, overthinking, and doubt reside—as we transition to the contentedness of being. There is both peace and power in relinquishing the need to control the details of our life and allowing our being to connect to the wisdom unfolding in the moment.

Perhaps no human in modern history has better recognized the healing power of awe than Dr. Victor Frankl, a preeminent twentieth-century psychiatrist and Holocaust survivor. In his groundbreaking book *Man's Search for Meaning*, Dr. Frankl recounts the shared awe experienced in the face of horrific suffering during his imprisonment in Auschwitz:[25]

> One evening, when we were already resting on the floor of our hut, dead tired, soup bowls in hand, a fellow prisoner rushed in and asked us to run out to the assembly grounds and see the wonderful sunset. Standing outside we saw sinister clouds glowing in the west and the whole sky alive with clouds of ever-changing shapes and colors, from steel blue to blood red. The desolate grey mud huts provided a sharp contrast, while the puddles on the muddy ground reflected the glowing sky. Then, after minutes of moving silence, one prisoner said to another, "How beautiful the world could be!"

Although he had experienced the unimaginable personal loss of his wife, mother, father, and brother and had endured the horrific attempt to strip away his humanity, Dr. Frankl survived and would go on to create Logotherapy. This is a psychotherapy that champions people's ability to choose purpose and meaning even in the worst of circumstances.

In a 1985 interview, Dr. Frankl poignantly described how it is possible to survive great suffering:[26]

> ...the essential lesson we all could learn is that survival (of horrific experiences) depends decisively on whether or not the respective individual was directed towards a future, toward a task waiting for him; a work to complete or for that matter to being reunited with a loved person. You may say this is hope. But it is more than hope because there is an automatic awareness implied and included. You have to give your best. You have to use this opportunity to turn it into something meaningful at the risk that it will all be in vain ... Each day has to be meaningful. That was our challenge ... Up onto the last breath, even in horrific circumstances, life retains meaning.

The shared moment of awe experienced by the entire population of the concentration camps was profound. As Dr. Frankl points out, the "meaning" element is what enables moments of awe to essentially connect us to our purpose.

When we experience a moment of awe, we are struck by this undeniable recognition that "life retains meaning" and we are part of something greater. This draws us forward, helping us engage with the understanding that meaning translates to purpose.

Uncovering Purpose by Zeroing In on Awe

Moments of awe are woven into our ordinary lives. Some are difficult to miss, but others require us to still our minds and absorb what is unfolding in our midst. As we determine to invite awe into our life, it is necessary to quiet our being and connect to the present moment.

Have you ever purchased a new car and then discovered that just about every other car on the highway is the one you bought? This is called the *frequency illusion*, and similar to seeing your car everywhere, you may notice awe all around you when you slow down and make room for Soul Chatter awareness.

In this chaotic world, setting an intention to experience awe will require a focused effort—this is mindfulness. In doing this, we make a conscious decision to release control of our mind center—our thinking, analyzing, and planning. Instead, we intend to *just be*. Consider this your Soul Chatter connection, the contented living-in-your-being that you may not realize you've been craving:

Slow down.

Take a deep belly-breath.

Connect to the songs of the world—the rain against your windowpane, a child's laughter, the bird's ballad. Posture yourself to experience this moment, knowing it will never come again. This moment is just for you—determine to savor it.

Big Picture Awe

We live in a breathtaking world. There are times when grandeur and magnificence are impossible to avoid, and we can't help but experience awe as it plays out on a grand scale right in front of us. This may occur in a private moment, or it could be shared with a group of people.

A simple moment of awe in my own life was when I became reacquainted with the magnificence of a tree. My first daughter was only a few weeks old when my husband and I decided to take her camping. We had just purchased a cool minivan. (I am aware of the oxymoron. But yes, minivans had their day!) We decided to cement our family reputation as wild and crazy adventure seekers by hitting the open road and taking our new baby camping.

Overriding the demands of our busy life, we hoped the unhurried pace of nature would provide needed respite. We found a perfect spot in the woods, parked our minivan, and unpacked the incredible amount of creature comforts we thought would be necessary to survive our night in the woods. I laid my sweet baby girl on her fuzzy blanket under the protection of a large tree.

Her eyes sparkled as she became mesmerized with the first tree she had ever seen—examining and memorizing every leaf as it swayed in the breeze. Watching this tiny human experience awe brought me awe as well. I gently lay on the ground next to her, and together we soaked in the sight.

I guess I had forgotten the complete and perfect awe in the simplicity of a tree. I was moved by the thought of a little seed producing branches, leaves, and bark out of water, dirt, and sunlight. The way a tree can create the oxygen we need to breathe from the carbon dioxide we expel has always perplexed me. That photosynthesis thing still blows my mind.

Zeroing In on Awe

We don't always experience awe as a thundering moment. We sometimes find it, instead, in a quiet, personal whisper. There are moments in our lives when we find ourselves becoming part of an unfolding plan, when it becomes apparent that random events could not possibly be orchestrated so perfectly.

Those are the times we do a double take and wonder, "Odd! How did that happen?" It might arrive in the form of something we desperately need—a person who suddenly calls or shows up at that exact right time. Or it could be a meaningful rhythm of events that only we know the nuance of, such as unexpected money showing up at an essential time or a sign that has the line we've been obsessing about. It might be an uncanny unfolding of a life-rhythm or a repeating pattern, like items that always land on their end when they are dropped. The orchestrated nature of personal awe can be a source of confirmation and can affirm meaning for a passion that has been nudging at our being.

An Awareness Story:
An Awesome Grape Nehi (Knee-Hi)

My life has been jam-packed with awe. Often, I've been too busy to recognize it—to stop and appreciate what was unfolding in front of me. An awe-moment that astounds me to this day took place during the summer of my junior year of high school.

I grew up in the small town of Laramie, Wyoming, the "Gem City of the Plains." (I never knew why it was known by this name—it's a rather glitzy description for a small western town.) It may be nostalgia, but life seemed more innocent then. Actually, as I question some of my adolescent choices, innocence may have saved my life a few times. Even so, I applaud the exuberance of my youth.

Perhaps due to sheer boredom, during one particular fit of impulsivity, my friend and I decided to hop on our bikes and ride to Centennial, a town at the base of the Snowy Range Mountains. It was a sixty-five-mile round trip.

We got so excited to make the trek that we literally took nothing for our journey, not even water. As you might expect, we were dry-mouth thirsty long before we reached our destination. Hopeful laughter soon turned to hanger as we began to realize we were not equipped for our self-imposed mission.

Still a couple of miles of hot asphalt left, we pulled our bikes to the shoulder of the road for a quick break. By this time, I had realized the tremendous importance of liquids, and I told my friend that I wished I had a grape Nehi. I have no idea why this particular drink popped into my head. It was an obscure brand of soda even then, and not something I usually drank. Acknowledging our need to trudge forward, we got back on our bikes and continued the ride.

A mile later, we stopped again, and I glanced at the ground. I could not believe what I saw. As requested, a single unopened can of grape Nehi was sitting on the shoulder of the road (I swear this is true). To say I was bewildered is an understatement. It was the most undeniable God-wink I have ever experienced.

There I stood, stunned, trying to understand how a single can of unopened grape Nehi could be undisturbed on the desolate plains of Wyoming. I was in *awe*. In my bemused state, I sat right there on the side of the road and accepted the gift. I popped the top of the can and took a big gulp. Hopeful laughter returned as my friend and I shared the rest of the can. Even though it was warm, I'm certain it was the best-tasting grape Nehi that has ever been drunk.

I have thought about my Nehi-moment many times since then because it reminds me to trust the process and resist the urge to control every detail of my life. Life unfolds in a profound way when I allow it. Controlling every detail of our lives not only gets in the way of miraculous outcomes but seriously tarnishes our outlook and attitude. Living life with tightly clenched fists does not allow for surprises and can be the thief of our joy.

It is important to be aware and notice when we find ourselves attempting to plan and polish each moment of our existence. We must occasionally let go of our desire to manage every moment. Understanding there are things we can control, but mindfully releasing what we cannot, is essential to joyfully living a passionate life.

Surprised by Personal Awe

We've all experienced moments when our needs are met so exactly that it demands our attention. These personal awe-moments are sometimes referred to as *Easter eggs* or *God-winks.* They are often life-changing. Like my grape Nehi experience, they are unique and knit into our journeys. Only our being center can process personal awe— it literally blows a connection in our mind center.

In a moment of personal awe, we witness life unfolding in such a specific way that it cannot be arbitrary. We feel a connection to something beyond ourselves, and it reinforces the understanding that there is a bigger plan to all the chaos we have been trudging around in. Take note and celebrate the uncanny order in the disorder.

Allow Your Life to Sparkle

Don't miss life unfolding all around you. There is awe residing just beyond the responsibilities and demands weighing you down and distracting you. There is a butterfly in your backyard ready to mesmerize you. In fact, you can find awe as close as your own hand—notice the intricacies in your skin and remember the stories behind your scars.

Close your eyes and take a deep cleansing breath. Connect to your surroundings with the wonder of a child. There is awe within your reach, right in this exact moment. You may have grown numb to awe and accepted the lie that your gifts and talents have no value. Or you may feel unsure of how to take the next step on your journey. There is a lot to unpack, and your journey continues. But for now, allow for a moment of wonder. I think Max Ehrmann expressed it best in his poem "Desiderata":[27]

> You are a child of the universe no less than the trees and the stars; you have a right to be here. And whether or not it is clear to you, no doubt the universe is unfolding as it should.

Purposeful Living
The Legacy of a Thoughtful Life

It is a privilege and a choice to ignite our passion. The message of passion flows through us and intersects with our purpose, bringing contentment to our being.

It matters. You matter.

Explore your gifts as you commit to purpose-guided living. Don't make this too complicated. Passionately living a purpose-filled life begins with the simple acceptance that you are.

Sozo Self-Connecting Exercise:
Awe-Infused Living

Intention: To bring awareness to your surroundings. Helpful for relaxing and delighting in the details.

Materials: Comfortable clothes and an uninterrupted, safe space. (Alternatively, you may go on a nature walk.)

Time: 15–20 minutes

Suggestion: Practice this daily for ten days. Make a habit of intentionally getting beyond your mind chatter.

Note: Pre-read the following directions so you can be present in the process as you experience it.

Begin with some connective breathwork to connect your nervous, gut, heart, and voice conscious centers.

Inhale. Breathe in through your nose, past your mind center, down your back, following your spine and filling your gut with clean air.

Exhale. Push the air up the front of your body, past your voice, and out your open mouth.

Repeat for seven to ten breaths.

Relax your body and be aware of your physical senses: breathing, hearing, and physical awareness.

Step 1

As you walk in nature or cozy up in your space, determine to orient yourself in the present moment. Use your senses to hear, see, and smell what is unfolding around you.

Start with your own hand. Look at the details—the color, the creases and pores, the way the light plays on its surface. Notice the imperfections and feel the texture. Experience your hand without judging it. Take time to notice how remarkable it is.

When you find your mind trying to taking over, reorient yourself to a *being-state*. Be intentional. Be aware.

Step 2

Choose another object to experience. It can be anything that calls your attention. Be aware of the details. Don't judge it; just drink in the color and texture. Connectively experience what is in front of you.

Again, work to continue in your being-state without letting your mind chatter intrude.

Step 3

Continue your walk or relax in your space. Experience other objects with a sense of present-moment awareness. Allow yourself to *be*. Recognize contentment as you connect with the awareness of awe at the tapestry of life being woven before you.

Purpose
What Next?

Our culture values mind chatter. The race for artificial intelligence highlights the current emphasis on excellent data processing. Yet the mystery of humanness is our ability to witness the nuance of our own thoughts and emotions from the serenity of our place of being. It is this present awareness that allows us to intentionally experience life as it unfolds and provides respite and restoration for our soul. Here we can connect to the wisdom of our Soul Chatter.

Holistic authenticity takes root as we deliberately respect our inner connection. Remember that this process is a journey and there is no single correct destination. By its very nature, there will be bumps in the road. The moment we feel comfortable being, our mind chatter—energized by our inner children—will have a temper tantrum, demanding our focus.

Overcoming the Obstacles to Disciplined Purpose
Enrolling Our Inner Children in Charm School

We innately understand that the passion and purpose awaiting us will require sacrifice and discipline. It's never a surprise what will happen next—our inner children will double down with fear-thoughts and distractions to slow our momentum. They prefer everything exactly as it is—stuck or not.

The elaborate game to preserve the status quo looks a lot like self-sabotage. Our inner children started scheming the moment we determined to pursue the possibilities tucked inside our hearts. We can expect this. It is part of the process. The next chapter will address the specific hindrances to self-harmonization and offer some suggestions for practical support.

There will be time to conquer hinderances, but for this moment, let's appreciate how far we've come in our Soul Chatter journey. It is never too late to say yes to our Soul Chatter's whispers.

Sozo Mini-Celebration:
A Well-Deserved Hug

Time: 1 solid minute

Supplies: Just yourself

Take a deep, intentional breath. As you breathe in, put each hand on your opposite upper arm. Squeeze yourself in a tight hug. Continue to squeeze and breathe as you embrace thoughts of love and appreciation for your inner children. Recognize how far you've come. Smile and allow positive feelings to envelop you.

When you are ready, throw your hands in the air and receive the empowerment and freedom of being you

Chapter Nine Notes

Step 6c: Sabotaging Self-Sabotage

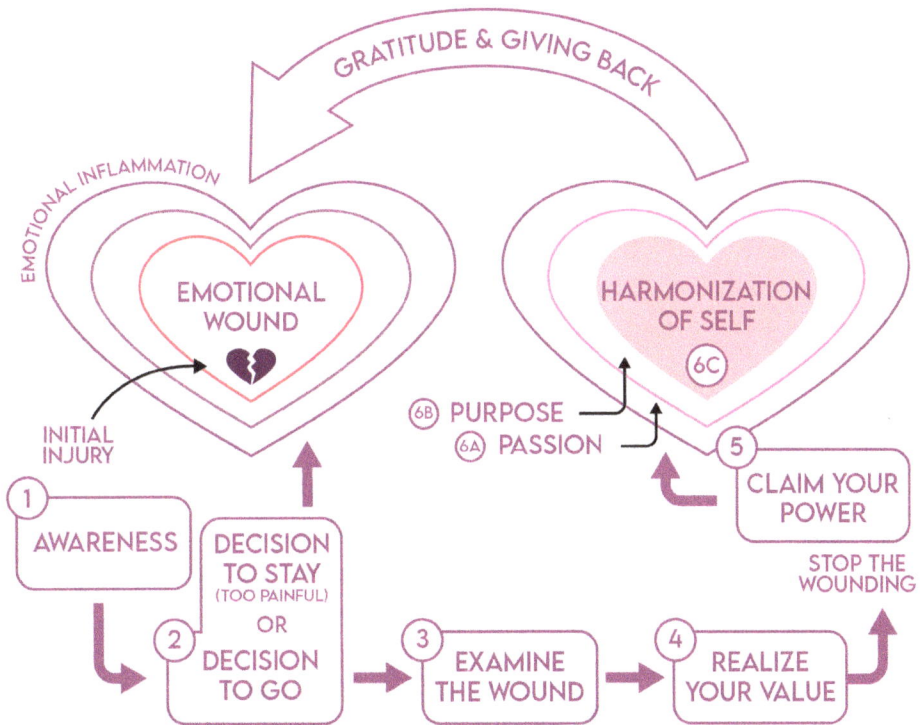

Corbett Model of Emotional Healing & Self-Integration™

We delight in the beauty of the butterfly, but rarely admit what it has gone through to achieve that beauty.[28]
—**Dr. Maya Angelou**

At this point on your self-harmonization journey, you may (rightly) feel like you have been pushing a boulder up a steep hill. You can see the dawn peeking over the horizon. It is so close yet just out of reach.

Soul Chatter fluency is the mastery of your inner connection. You become conscious of the changes in yourself and mindfully balance your thinking, feeling, and being. You look forward to the contentment and freedom of authentic living:

- As soon as you complete that project you have been working on.

- As soon as you finish that course you have been studying.

- As soon as your kids grow up.

- As soon as you get the approving nod from your mentor or the wink and pat on the back from your BFF.

- As soon as you can forgive _____ for hurting you.

- As soon as you can embrace your inner children and respect how they react to emotional pain.

The demands of life are ever present, and meeting them can be daunting. It may be helpful to take a short pause on your journey to assess your efforts, celebrate your victories, and plan your next move. The truth is that life is messy and rarely follows our planned script.

Take a moment to honestly evaluate the hindrances that may be blocking you from living your best life. Next, we will explore those stumbling blocks and consider practical countermeasures for holding your ground when you notice behaviors or habits that trip you up. You didn't think I was going to leave you stranded at the crest of the mountain, did you?

A Life Story: Confessions of a Self-Saboteur
Hold My Wine as I Share My Sabotage Story

The life story that I originally planned to share with you in this chapter was a tale of a well-coiffed, successful client who struggled with self-sabotage. But as I began to recount her struggles, it became apparent that the best illustration I have is of my own personal hindrances. I had been doing the very thing in my own life that I was so resolutely intending to help you avoid.

Hold my wine.

Growing up, I often heard my mother tell me I was fearless and exotic. I believed her, and I clung to that identity. I was a quiet but bold young girl. Childhood memories flash before me—I see myself standing and observing the world around me, knowing I have a part in it. I was certain I was put on earth for a purpose. The specifics of that objective were never clear to me, but I knew it came with an eclectic set of talents and passions.

Throughout my life, my diverging talents have occasionally intersected and made for something audacious and glorious. Unfortunately (and all too often), on the edge of triumph is where self-sabotage rears its rather hideous head.

Recently, I found myself treading murky water, enduring a feeding frenzy of old and comfortable fear-thoughts—but this time with a new, more lethal twist. I've spent decades conquering the soundtracks of perfection and the fear of living a life of mediocrity. [29]

Thought patterns on the road to self-sabotage are lethal, because they work. Our inner children know what makes us tick, and in their efforts to protect us from emotional pain, they often leave us frozen in our tracks.

My recent paralyzing thought pattern was one I'd never considered before. I was not exactly sure how to diffuse it. It whispered, "What do you think you're going to do next? You've used up all your magic, and you're all out of tricks." That was rude—but partially true. I had achieved the dream of my young self, and now my future was unclear.

Had my life passions already played out? How many times can I begin the next great adventure? What do you do when you reach a stage of life that is beyond what you had dreamt for yourself?

As a young girl growing up in Laramie, I aspired to be an architect. My plan was to live in a high-rise in Chicago (I have no idea why), drive a red Corvette, and own an Afghan hound. Something about that image enticed me, and I set out to make it happen. Decades later, I am thrilled to report that not one of those early dreams came to fruition, except for the Afghan hound—which I later learned is a poor choice of dog for a Chicago high-rise, but that's another story.

After several years, I matured a bit, met my patient, gentle husband, and revised my life goals. My new dream was to be an entrepreneur and design ways to help people improve their lives. I planned to have a family and to go on many adventures with them, encouraging one other and sprinkling in a lot of spontaneous laughter along the way. In my own way and in my own style, I desired to take any of life's lemons and make the best damn glass of lemonade that anyone ever tasted.

Over the next few decades, I checked all the boxes on my dream list as time flew by. And yes, time does fly. As my youngest son went off to college with his own set of big dreams and my two daughters started families of their own, I paused to contemplate my life and wipe away an occasional sentimental tear. I observed that our once bustling nest was inescapably empty.

Perhaps even more disheartening was the realization that I had already lived the life I envisioned for myself. I had never seriously contemplated my life beyond this point.

Simultaneously celebrating the achievement of my dreams and panicking about the uncertainty of what to do next is the most emotionally dualistic experience I have ever had. My twenty-four-year-old middle daughter came home for Thanksgiving and put her snarky assessment of our life on social media: "Judging from my parents' pantry (just pancake mix, margarita salt, and canned green chili) empty nesting is just a repeat of your 20s."

In the midst of my ensuing meltdown, I turned over the wheel to one of my inner children, the one who loves to ensure I am organized. She believes her contribution is to save the day by preventing me from doing something "crazy" or embarrassing. (Like that has ever happened!) She has perfected these fear-thoughts over the years.

As a wellness advocate, I am intimately familiar with rebuffing fear-thoughts, reworking patterns, and employing tools (sabo-tools) to get back on track, yet my *stinkin'-thinkin'* playlist was set on a continuous loop. Not only had I allowed my chatty inner children to throw a rager, but I had joined them at the party by throwing in a few of my own fainthearted cheers.

When I am undone, one of my go-to self-soothing techniques is to recount each and every possible scenario to help me fully understand the best way out of my predicament. This is a surefire way to drive all my loved ones absolutely nuts. Their eyes glaze over as I incessantly obsess over the issue du jour.

I have come to realize that this method of working through my issues is not the best prescription for personal joy or flourishing relationships. But, speaking for all of us who occasionally wallow in *poor me* mud, sometimes the march through hell seems to require a quick dip in the self-pity pond. The danger is that you often get a bit more stuck than you intended.

Several months passed as I sunk deeper and grew comfortable in the deep shadowy abyss of self-doubt. Then, one Sunday afternoon in early spring, I told myself that a certain project was too difficult to attempt. In a fit of negativity, I concluded, *I could never do that. It's too hard.* Too hard? That was the finger-snap I needed to get me out of my mind chatter. I recollected an old familiar mantra: "Do the hard things. You were made to do the hard things."

I literally gasped as this truth jolted me. I couldn't recall ever shying away from something I felt passionate about just because it seemed too difficult. Why would I start now? What I know to be true of myself is that, if I feel passionately about something, I will do it. Frankly, I don't really care who tells me otherwise.

It became clear to me that I had arrived at the crest of my mountain, and it was time to quit rerunning scenarios in my head or getting stuck in a funhouse of fear. I needed to reconnect with the wisdom of my Soul Chatter and *be*. I had become stuck, waiting for someone to step up and connect the dots in my life. I did not need anyone's permission or stamp of approval to move forward with my personal commitment to do the hard things.

Sometimes it's necessary to pivot. We can choose to reject the fear that keeps us stuck. This is similar to beginning the next chapter of a book you're already reading: you are familiar with the characters, the setting, and the genre—now it's time to navigate the plot twist.

I have lived my life jumping into the deep ends of frigid pools and allowing my passions to take me to unexpected places. I didn't balk then, and I won't now. The next chapter of my life story might be wild, weird, or rather tame. I haven't completely decided. But there is one thing that I am certain of: the next chapter of my story is mine to write. Neither the critics nor my inner fear-chorus gets to change the narrative. Perhaps it will be a romantic comedy with an adventurous heroine who deeply loves her people and moonlights as a beekeeper. Who knows?

Recognizing Those Joy Stealers
Drop-Kicking Hindrances and Embracing Joy

Simply put, the journey to self-harmonization is getting back to yourself. But you and I both know it's not always that easy. There are many hindrances that fly in the face of our best intentions. We can learn a great deal from studying time-tested methods for conquering obstacles.

Throughout human history, many remarkable people have dedicated themselves to authentic living. Thought leaders, religious teachers, and modern-day psychological researchers have wrestled with how to help humans remove the barriers that keep us from attaining our greatest potential. I have highlighted some of the classic methods so that we can glean from their experience.

- Gautama Buddha: In his quest to provide a clear path to mindfulness and meditation, he identified negative mental states that may hinder personal progress and suggested antidotes.

- Judeo-Christians: In an effort to gain control over the slippery slope of the seven deadly sins, religious adherents have employed the practice of integrating their corresponding virtues.

- Monastic traditions: From the third century on, desert fathers and mothers have dedicated their lives to methods of self-inquiry, prayer, and self-denial.

- Modern-day psychology has developed a myriad of theories and therapies but leans heavily on mindfulness and present-moment awareness to calm overthinking and stress that accompanies contemporary living.

I fully recognize that, in my effort to glean from those who have gone before me, I have oversimplified these complex practices and lost a great deal of their essence. My goal with this overview is to formulate practices that respect the reality of time-tested traditions. In comparing these methodologies that aim to identify and curb self-sabotaging behaviors, there are some common threads that may be helpful in tackling obstacles in our own self-harmonization journey.

Hindrances to Self-Harmonization

The Predicament and Its Antidote

Consider the irony—it takes intentional effort and energy to become who we already are. Why does a life that looks so effortlessly authentic require so much effort? Perhaps that is why people who have the courage to pursue this path stand out—they sparkle.

Each of the methods I have highlighted for overcoming hinderances have something in common. They are all ways to self-mastery and to letting go of the distractions that derail us from our journey. They all require discipline and intentionality.

Incorporating mindfulness into our daily lives sounds like a great idea, but the necessary persistence and focus can be tedious and lonely. Despite the challenges, the reward of present awareness is authentically living a life that answers the call of our Soul Chatter.

The following guide is an inventory of common roadblocks and their countermeasures. The following chart considers and combines multiple practices for overcoming mental, emotional, and spiritual barriers—including Buddhist, Judeo-Christian, and psychological methods and their corresponding corrective actions.

How to Use This Guide

This guide is designed to help you examine five of the classic emotional and mental states and how they are currently affecting your life journey. As you familiarize yourself with the obstacles, contemplate each one separately and ask yourself, "Is this an issue in my life worthy of consideration?" If you feel that it isn't, be grateful and move on to the next. If you know, or even suspect, that it is, then take time for a self-inventory. Evaluate how that vice might lure you out of your place of strength. How does that obstacle attach to you? And what purpose does it serve?

It may be that the hindrance we find most alluring has become habitual. On some level our personal rebellion against a positive outcome might bump against a deep fear. We could view it as an inner child's efforts to protect us from a perceived pain.

The following chart identifies five types of obstacles, along with their suggested corrective actions, viewed through the lens of each practice—psychological (mind state), philosophical (Buddhist), and spiritual (Judeo-Christian virtue). You may want to make a regular practice of looking through the obstacles, as your vulnerabilities will change over time.

When using this chart, begin with the end in mind. As you identify which issue may be keeping you stuck, be mindful of how the vice may hinder your personal journey and notice when those dynamics begin to take root in your life. And consider employing the corresponding counter-step that most resonates with you. It may be helpful to keep a list of the corrections and to intentionally practice them on a regular basis.

Best-Life Predicament and Correction Checklist

OBSTACLE / PREDICAMENT	CORRECTION
Mind State #1: Attachment energy / Addiction	Mindful Energy: Consistent routines, Healthy support systems
Hindrance #1: Desire for Sense Pleasure	Antidote: Contentment and Awareness
Sin #1: Gluttony, Greed	Virtue: Moderation, Generosity
Mind State #2: Anger/ Fire Energy, Frustration, Fear of Inadequacy, Disconnection	Softening Energy: Self-compassion, Affirmation, Parts work, and Self Harmonization
Hindrance #2: Ill Will, Aversion, Anger	Antidote: Unity / Compassion
Sin #2: Anger, Envy	Virtue: Patience, Kindness
Mind State#3: Cloudy /Depressed Energy	Increasing Energy: Sparking, Positive Scripts & Self Care Behaviors
Hindrance #3: Sloth and Torpor	Antidote: Joyful attitude, Aspiration, Positive Thinking
Sin #3: Sloth/Apathy	Virtue: Diligence
Mind State #4: Restless Energy, Agitated - Anxiety	Consistent Energy: Present moment and awareness practices
Hinderance #4: Restlessness / Worry - Monkey Mind	Antidote: Mindfulness
Sin #4: Lust	Virtue: Chastity/Abstinence
Mind State #5: Inadequacy, helplessness	Cultivate Self Awareness, positivity, Empowerment
Hinderance #5: Doubt	Recognize the negative energy and refocus on the positive.
Sin #5: Pride	Humility, Faith

Obstacle #1: Overindulging Our Senses

The first obstacle to consider is the desire to engage our bodily senses. Our senses are how we perceive and communicate with the world around us. They are a beautiful part of living, but we can overindulge them. Thus, the very thing that connects us becomes our path to numbing or disassociation.

Overindulgence of sensory pleasure can become such a strong obsession that we are eventually willing to give up everything else to soak it in. On a physical level, we can indulge addictions that flood our brain with pleasure-inducing chemicals, which provide us with a huge hit we can't find anywhere else. Then we crave that flood of feeling again and continue to seek that high. Essentially, our desire for that sensation in our brain becomes our god, and we relinquish control of our actions.

OBSTACLE / PREDICAMENT	CORRECTION
Mind State #1: Attachment energy / Addiction	Mindful Energy: Consistent routines, Healthy support systems
Hindrance #1: Desire for Sense Pleasure	Antidote: Contentment and Awareness
Sin #1: Gluttony, Greed	Virtue: Moderation, Generosity

Be Aware

Those little screens in our pockets, social media, and corporate marketing generate massive profits by projecting emotion onto objects. There are entire industries devoted to influencing our wishes and catering to our desires.

A designer bag may make us feel wealthy, and a hot romantic partner may make us feel valuable. But who we are and how we feel is not determined by what we have or who we know. Objectifying people or personalizing objects is a false dichotomy and will never produce authentic contentment or real connections.

Antidote

The antidote to the first obstacle (our desire to indulge our senses) is to live with moderation. In other words, we should be aware of our personal vulnerabilities, find accountability, and maintain a vigilant perspective when engaging with the specific objects or experiences that entice us. For example, a good glass of wine or a small piece of black forest cake can be enjoyed without polishing off the bottle or eating the entire cake.

Or we may conclude that some things tempt us so much that we must avoid engaging with them completely. Instead, we can seek healthy substitutes, such as delighting in a breathtaking sunset or a genius work of art without possessing them.

Obstacle #2: Anger

The second obstacle is excessive anger. This is a result of focusing on what frustrates or annoys us. When we indulge fierce emotions with toxic thinking, it taints our positivity and leads to the destruction of people, places, things, and eventually our own being. It is the extinction of hope.

It's important to recognize that feeling angry is normal. Experiencing the full range of our emotions is fully living. The problem is not the emotions we feel but what we choose to do with those feelings. When we choose to stew in anger, we can become locked in toxic rage. The choice to fixate on our fury becomes central and leads us into a downward spiral.

OBSTACLE / PREDICAMENT	CORRECTION
Mind State #2: Anger / Fire Energy, Frustration, Fear of Inadequacy, Disconnection	Softening Energy: Self-compassion, Affirmation, Parts work, and Self Harmonization
Hindrance #2: Ill Will, Aversion, Anger	Antidote: Unity / Compassion
Sin #2: Anger, Envy	Virtue: Patience, Kindness

Example

Everyday living carries a host of unwelcome experiences. In our tech-savvy culture, rampant doomscrolling and social polarization contributes to divisions and diversions that shadow our joy. The intentional practice of compassion and unity is a space of grace we can offer as our contribution to a more peaceful world.

Be Aware

Many people have difficulty expressing emotion—they consider sadness a sign of weakness, while anger is considered acceptable. Consequently, many people bottle up their emotions, leaving them unprocessed. When they finally explode, everything gets released as anger.

Anger is powerful, and indulging it quickly becomes a spreading fire we can no longer extinguish. Anger, fury, and rage are intense, fiery emotions that can form an obsessive connection to the person or object we despise.

Antidote

Anger is just the tip of the spear, and the underlying emotions are often sadness, fear, and shame. Having the courage to tease out and process the emotions behind the fury will help defuse the rage-bomb. Developing an understanding of our own emotional makeup and setting an intention to practice unconditional love is our avenue to Soul Chatter contentment.

Obstacle #3: Lethargy of the Mind and Inactivity of the Body

The third obstacle is lack of motivation. This mental and physical manifestation is a slow descent into hopelessness and disconnection from our struggles, but also from our passions and joys. The result is apathy, which dulls our energy and numbs our mind.

OBSTACLE / PREDICAMENT	CORRECTION
Mind State #3: Cloudy / Depressed Energy	Increasing Energy: Sparking, Positive Scripts & Self Care Behaviors
Hindrance #3: Sloth and Torpor	Antidote: Joyful attitude, Aspiration, Positive Thinking
Sin #3: Sloth / Apathy	Virtue: Diligence

Example

There are times when every human experiences the depressed energy and apathy that accompanies a feeling of hopelessness. It is easy to want to give up. Recognizing and promptly addressing apathy is important so it does not become a stronghold. This obstacle is sad to witness in a person we care about. To see others lose their passion is difficult—we cannot draw them out of their apathy, so we feel helpless to respond.

Be Aware

Often, slothfulness doesn't happen because we don't care. It can even be the opposite: we care deeply but just feel like we have no control over a situation. When we have pushed ourselves beyond our limits, indifference can be the trap. It's important to realize you are not an apathetic or lazy person, but you may have developed apathetic or lazy habits. You can choose your destiny and resist the labels other people may try to tag you with.

Antidote

Life ebbs and flows in a rhythmic fashion. There are seasons to rest and rejuvenate and others to grow. It is imperative we stay mindful and not remain in one place just because it feels comfortable. We should intentionally focus on positive thinking and what sparks joy. Committing to routines and self-care is also essential.

Obstacle #4: A Restless Mind and Anxiousness

The fourth obstacle is the restless state that results in an anxious, unsettled mind. This obstacle is often described as *monkey mind* because of the intellect's tendency to swing from branch to branch, distracted and easily influenced by the chaos of the surrounding jungle.

The result of this mind state is mental exhaustion and a lack of peace. Our intellect has become spoiled and undisciplined. It refuses to take a back seat to mindfulness or present-moment awareness.

OBSTACLE / PREDICAMENT	CORRECTION
Mind State #4: Restless Energy, Agitated - Anxiety	Consistent Energy: Present moment and awareness practices
Hinderance #4: Restlessness / Worry - Monkey Mind	Antidote: Mindfulness
Sin #4: Lust	Virtue: Chastity / Abstinence

Example

The chaos of the outside world profits from stimulating our lustful desires for the next shiny thing. Lifestyle choices can set us up for success or drain our reserves. Take a moment to examine your habits.

Do you have poor sleep hygiene (lack of sleep or distractions to sleep), poor nutrition (too much sugar or poor overall dietary choices), or addictions to stimulants or drugs (including abused prescriptions)? If your lifestyle includes, say, three energy drinks per day (even sugar-free ones), too much multitasking, or other unhealthy choices, you may be setting yourself up for a very hard climb.

Be Aware

Stress is the most common issue that brings people in for outpatient therapy. The unrealistic expectations and constant stimulation fueled by technology make mindfulness and present-moment living less of a priority. The real anxiety that results from mental, physical, and emotional stress may be the silent pandemic of our times.

Antidote

Mindfulness and consistency are powerful antidotes to the hindrance of an unsettled mind. Present-moment-living practices can be incorporated into everyday routines. A balanced lifestyle is an essential foundation for achieving peace of mind and conquering the hindrance of restless thinking and agitation.

Obstacle #5: Doubt

The fifth obstacle is fear and doubt. This state of mind can be paralyzing since it stops us from enjoying our choices and moving forward. The inability to feel strength in our identity and our beliefs chips away at our confidence and decision-making.

OBSTACLE / PREDICAMENT	CORRECTION
Mind State #5: Inadequacy, helplessness	Cultivate Self Awareness, positivity, Empowerment
Hinderance #5: Doubt	Recognize the negative energy and refocus on the positive.
Sin #5: Pride	Humility, Faith

Example

In our society, fear and conflicting messages are rampant. There is a multitude of easily accessible opinions and advice, yet very little of it has our best interest at heart. It is easy to attach ourselves to manicured identities and digital personas as a way of feeling in control. This inauthenticity eventually leads to doubt and inadequacy.

Be Aware

We can be certain that our authentic choices will be challenged and our unique message will be critiqued. It takes a great deal of resolve to consider advice without getting lost in it. Our ability to trust our Soul Chatter wisdom will strengthen us to stand firm in uncertain times.

Antidote

You can make a practice of engaging in mindful self-awareness and positive thinking. Do this by recognizing when doubt and negativity are encroaching on your thoughts and consciously replace them with a positive script. Connect to your passions and remember your uniqueness. Refuse to believe the lie that your life can only be enjoyed after it's become flawless.

Sozo Exercise:
Removing Obstacles to Self-Harmonization

Conscious Connection: Employing the Antidote
Love Thyself—Mind, Body, and Spirit

This reflective exercise is helpful for removing habits that hinder you from authentic living.

<u>Materials</u>: Your journal, a pen, and the Obstacle Checklist.

Take a deep breath, in through your nose and out through your mouth. As you breathe, relax your body and still your mind. Take a moment and sink into your being-state. Meditate, pray, or visualize your life as content. Connect to your Soul Chatter by intentionally calming your mind chatter and bringing your emotional state into the present.

Next, browse the Obstacle Checklist and identify which hindrances resonate most with you. On a scale of 1–10 (with 1 being not at all and 10 being to an extreme extent), mentally rate the degree to which each of them allures you. Scrutinize the one with the highest rating and consider how it affects your life. Considering the future, where will this hindrance take you if left unchecked? How will it affect your life? Is the impact desirable?

This is slippery slope awareness, a method of recognizing the extent to which a habit may take you to a point of self-sabotage or harm. How close can you get to the edge of the cliff before this hindrance pushes you over? Once you are aware of that boundary, you can avoid engaging in that harmful behavior.

Note: Unless you care to jump off the wagon entirely, you will need to have an alternate plan or a substitute behavior to support you in the effort to stay focused and on track.

If you decide you are *not* willing to live with the projection of this hindrance, find the courage to address it. Study the antidote and find ways to incorporate it into your life. If, at this time, you can bear the consequences of this hindrance, then accept them as a part of your current pattern and consider revisiting this exercise when you are ready.

Authentic Living

The Grace of Self-Acceptance

One of the most fulfilling legs of the self-harmonization journey is navigating the very space we've been avoiding. This is where we allow mistakes and release control, trusting that life will unfold as it should. It's where we accept—and occasionally celebrate—the awe-inspiring messiness of life.

Self-harmonization is a way of living that requires perseverance, course correction, and acceptance of and compassion for ourselves. This is the recipe for being good parents to our inner children. Imagine validating that dejected part of us that doesn't feel worthy of love. Visualize the freedom of self-acceptance and the joy of living without self-judgment. In this place we:

- simultaneously affirm the reality of our insignificance and the importance of our purpose.

- accept adversity yet persevere.

- love people well while enforcing healthy boundaries.

In the next chapter we will look at the specifics regarding the self-harmonization of our inner children.

Chapter Ten Notes

CHAPTER ELEVEN

Harmonization of Self

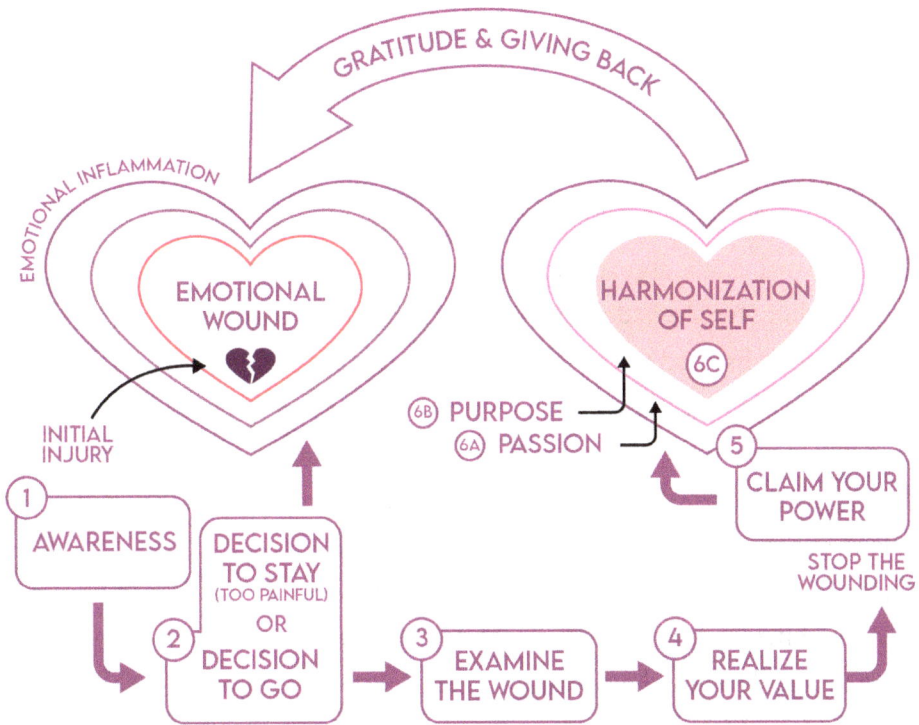

Corbett Model of Emotional Healing & Self-Integration™

> I shall be telling this with a sigh
> Somewhere ages and ages hence:
> Two roads diverged in a wood, and I—
> I took the one less traveled by,
> And that has made all the difference.[30]
> **—Robert Frost**

The Importance of Loving Your Inner Children
Appreciating Your Inner Rebel

One of my mother's favorite stories took place when I was a rebellious preteen. I had just learned the power of the middle finger and decided to employ it from the back seat of my grandmother's Thunderbird. Unfortunately, the receiver of my message recognized the car and followed us to our next stopping point.

There, she painstakingly explained to my mother and grandmother my "shocking" behavior, adding that she had voted for my grandmother in the last school board election. My mother listened to the woman through gritted teeth while flashing me the wait-until-we-get-home glare. She was mortified and felt judged as an inadequate mother. When the woman had finished her story and returned to her car, my grandmother laughed hysterically, then leaned over to my mother and quipped, "I never dreamed I would get so even."

That memory came scurrying back to my mind recently, prompted by a toddler who declared her independence by full-body bathing in a puddle in front of an upscale restaurant. That child was basking in the I-don't-care freedom we all experience less and less as responsibilities, obligations, and reputations become our drivers.

Perhaps you no longer desire to bathe in puddles (or maybe you do), but most of us can relate to the desire to break free of the expectations the world uses to inhibit our actions and extract joy from our lives.

I now can report that, after many years of working with my inner rebel, she has matured and gained a modicum of self-control. But she is still unmatched when it comes to sparking up the next great adventure.

When was the last time you felt the freedom to embrace your dance-like-nobody's-watching life? Consider connecting with your inner rebel and letting them drive the car for a few miles on this leg of your journey. No longer a rebellious teenager, they might now have some wisdom to share. Unleash that cheetah scarf or free the tartan necktie from the depths of the bottom drawer, and rock it at work.

The Paradigm Shift

All of us have conflicting parts. You might think, *A part of me wants to quit my job, and another part of me thinks it would be a good idea to stay because it has good benefits.* It might be easier to characterize those conflicting parts if you consider them to be your inner children.

Our inner children have reasons for projecting the way they do, and although they may be misguided, they are usually trying to do what they consider best for us. Our Soul Chatter journey is the experience of becoming familiar with and connecting to our own being.

This is the process of peeling away the superficial and leaning on our awareness and intuition. It is the pursuit of an authentic understanding of the nuances that make up our own persona. Courageous self-examination is the only way we can commit to fully living a life of integrity and passion.

At some point during the process of self-harmonization, what is important becomes crystal clear. Letting go of obstacles and making a necessary coarse correction produces the focus and energy required to pivot toward an authentic life of integrity. It is time to calm the inner conflict and declare peace among your parts with self-acceptance and love.

It's difficult, but people can and do make changes. Claiming your life, authoring your story, and living a life that is true to your narrative—these are important steps to self-harmonization. At this point, you may decide you are happy with your current trek and radical changes are no longer necessary. Congratulations! You can celebrate and lean into your current life.

The Pivot

Occasionally, there are moments of clarity when you realize your current path is not going to get you to the place you long to be. Perhaps it is time to consider ways to pivot or retool some of your choices. A life pivot can be small;-you may not need to make radical changes to live a life that energizes your passions. Remember those small course corrections? They get you to a whole new destination on the other side of your journey. If, when, and to what degree you pivot is always your choice.

One of these pivots was illustrated through Robin Williams's role in the movie *World's Greatest Dad*. Williams has long been one of my favorite actors. His life was brilliant, and we can all agree the world was a better place when he was in it. He had a genius understanding of emotional depth and how to tap into it. Over his career, Williams's earlier comedic slapstick characters, like Mork from Ork or Genie in *Aladdin*, gave way to more emotionally sophisticated roles that provided a glimpse into life's deepest struggles.

In *World's Greatest Dad*, Williams's character, Lance Clayton, is a portrait of a man who has settled. He has quit chasing his dreams and has taken the people-pleasing path of least resistance. But after a tragic loss, Lance fully comprehends the lie he has been living and chooses to pivot. In a burst of Soul Chatter freedom, he claims his life on his own terms.

He begins his new, authentic chapter by announcing his truth to a packed room of his so-called friends and colleagues. He declares, "I used to think the worst thing in life was to end up all alone. It's not. The worst thing in life is ending up with people who make you *feel* all alone."[31] Boom! Lance is no longer willing to live a lie. The room falls silent in slack-jawed amazement as he delivers his truth.

Lance then inaugurates his soul-soaring freedom by flatlining a slight smile before walking away. He gradually picks up speed until he is sprinting down the hall toward the high school swimming pool. Piece by piece, he rips off each article of his clothing—buttons popping off—and hurls them on the ground.

He claims his victory as he triumphantly climbs the ladder to the high dive and baptizes himself into his authentic life by swan-diving into the pool, wearing nothing but his knee-high blue socks. With that dive, Lance has let go of all the hindrances and has chosen to pivot and become the author of his own story.

A Life Story
The Art of Living

As I perused my mental Rolodex for a person who lived a self-harmonized life, I immediately thought of my friend, Baron Batch. Our unlikely friendship has been cemented by our mutual desire to help others and give back to our community.

I first met Baron when we co-hosted a party at one of my juice stores. He sauntered in with an entourage. I smiled at his colorful paint-splattered jeans, which gave off the perfect artist vibe. His calm, assured demeanor energized and attracted the crowd. He was both fearlessly detached and thoughtfully present. I would later learn that Baron is also a generous person who prioritizes radical giving.

Baron has wholeheartedly lived a multidimensional life, beginning with his childhood in Midland, Texas. He reminisced that even back then he was an observer. In *A Harmonious Life*, a documentary short film about his journey, he says, "From where I was when I was younger, there was definitely a level of discontent. It forces you to be outwardly focused. You think what is out there is going to change how you feel inside. Art was something that helped me do that because it was something that came from within me."

Baron's athleticism led his journey to College Station, where he played football for Texas A&M, and eventually to Pittsburgh to play professionally for the Steelers. "The greatest thing you can achieve," he says of going pro is, "if you are not spiritually healthy and mentally healthy—that's still a loss. It took away the kid in me." That realization translated to his next transition, which was a return to the awareness he had as a young man. He began his evolution toward a respected artist of both paint and word.

Life's twists and turns are never as random as we imagine. The 2020 pandemic, for instance, forced many people into isolation. During that period, Baron retreated to his studio and worked to keep his health commitments, partially supported by having juice packs delivered from one of my stores.

On several occasions, I had the opportunity to drop them off personally and touch base with Baron. It was always inspiring to observe his artistic process and the atmosphere of his creative hideaway. Baron's working studio is an extension of his art: intensity of color and assurance of patterns provide a foundation for playful excursions of artistic experimentation.

Large graffiti-esque canvases line the walls precisely depicting movement with humorous splatters of bold color. There were times when I visited Baron and he had playfully assigned a persona to his studio. On one of those occasions, he had worked in a Batman theme, complete with a mask displayed on a shelf. This gave him an opportunity to interact with his muse and further solidify his message.

Baron reflected, "It is not that we are to look to be inspired—for in doing this we can quickly become distracted from what is always with us—but to remember that we are that. May we realize that within each breath we are gifted. Our very existence is inspiration, and through our very existence, we create. So, the question is not what inspires. The inquiry is, what are you choosing to breathe life into? Through you, what is brought to life?"[32]

In the years I have known him, Baron's dreams and schemes have never wavered, and his story continues as one of inner awareness, harmony, and gratitude. True to his character, Baron has never pretended that his journey was without struggles or roadblocks.

Yet, while overcoming, his journey of conscious living allows him to retain the colorful, present-moment optimism that is undeniably visible through the lens of his art. He has harmonized the nuanced pieces of his character and has allowed each to have its voice—the dedication and awareness of a professional athlete, the wonderment and innocence of a young boy from Texas, and the creative savvy of an entrepreneur. The genius of the whole is his ability to respect and harmonize the parts.

Baron's harmonization of self is apparent in his dogged pursuit of the passions that lead to his purpose. His gratitude and generosity have become his hallmark, punctuated by his #FREE art drops.

Over the years, he has gifted a multitude of his work to his supporters and strangers by placing his paintings out on the street and posting it on social media with #FREE. Baron believes his art is not his to possess and has inspired countless people by his acts of gratitude and giving back. "It simply goes through me for other people to enjoy."

As we trust the wisdom of our Soul Chatter, we become comfortable with the paradox of our parts. We can embrace our present space, being simultaneously powerful and nothing, while understanding that both carry huge burdens and risks.

One of the greatest challenges of being a self-harmonized human is reconciling the multitude of opposing desires and accessing the myriad of talents whirling within our earthly bodies. Being raw and real about who we are requires that we embrace the totality of our parts—even the quirky inner children we have been ignoring—while respecting the wisdom of our being self.

This might require us to intentionally temper our perfectionist inner critic while giving voice to our playful or rebellious side in our daily routine. Or, if we have been letting our inner rebel choose our itinerary, it may be time to allow our practical inner child to set our agenda. The practice of Soul Chatter fluency for self-harmonization requires that we:

- reduce our mind chatter,

- calm our emotional energy,

- engage our Soul Chatter,

- acknowledge and respect the diversity of our parts,

- and, finally, employ the grace of self-acceptance (the ultimate act of self-care).

Reduce Your Mind Chatter
Understanding Your Spoiled Mind

We know a great deal about the structure of the human brain. Psychiatry, behavioral science, and clinical research have made strides toward providing greater access to positive mental health, healing from trauma, and well-being practices. As a mental health provider, I am proud of my colleagues for their dedication to furthering the science and craft of emotional wellness.

Yet, for all our research, the complexities of the human mind are not always as predictable or explainable as we would hope. The experience of societal trauma has propelled the stress epidemic. Most of my outpatient clients list anxiety as a major component of their initial complaint. With the stimulation of screens and endless communication threads, incessant thinking has become the norm.

Our mind chatter forces its way into the driver seat of our life choices. We have become a society of mentally exhausted people, which not only leads to physical issues but, sadly, also steals our joy. We are so busy thinking that we forget to live.

There are some very successful techniques and therapies specifically designed to slow incessant thinking and promote mindfulness and trauma work. If you are still struggling with any of these issues and believe these therapies would be helpful, I recommend you enlist a therapist who is trained to assist you in releasing past pain and further developing mindful practices.

On a practical level, mind chatter is countered with living real life in real time. If we can focus on our passions and become mesmerized by the awe of the moment, present-moment living will prevail, and our minds will lose the power to nag us.

Calm Your Emotional Energy
You Are Not Your Feelings

We are emotional creatures. The power that resides within us in the form of emotional energy is a wonderful tool but is too often misunderstood. Just like mind chatter, emotional energy is only part of the picture and cannot become a dictator if we hope to live a balanced life.

Consider our emotions our sensory data collector, a helpful meter for understanding the possibilities and dangers of the world around us. Emotions are essential for gaining an accurate awareness of our environment, but some of the data collected with our emotional barometer may require further analysis before taking action. What we believe to be true, as told by our emotions, may need to be tempered with Soul Chatter wisdom.

The ability to interpret emotional energy accurately is innate, but it can be further developed or dulled. One interesting pattern I've observed when working with clients is that many people who are emotionally intelligent and have the ability to decode relational dynamics are hesitant to use their gifts because they are uncomfortable with their own emotional state. They believe the safety of being cerebral will allow them to avoid emotional vulnerability. But in truth, mindfully accessing emotions is an essential step to connect authentically with other people and ourselves.

Engage Your Soul Chatter
Connecting with Your Being-Self

Soul Chatter fluency is a state of peaceful, grounded self-connection. We can hone our self-grounding techniques by intentionally calming our mind chatter and allowing our emotions to rise up and float away. This stillness in the moment strengthens our ability to be wholly present.

Present-moment consciousness without an agenda initially feels uncomfortable and for this reason, we may have been avoiding a Soul Chatter connection most of our lives. But in this state, we're able to tap into our intuition and more accurately sense the relationship dynamics of the people around us.

Incorporating mindful practices into everyday living helps balance mind chatter and calm emotions. These practices transform our thinking processes and even produce physical changes in our brains. Studies conducted on mindfulness practices illustrate the adaptation of the physical brain as it restructures to support continued "higher order brain functions":

> MRI scans show that after an eight-week course of mindfulness practice, the brain's "fight or flight" center, the amygdala, appears to shrink. This primal region of the brain, associated with fear and emotion, is involved in the initiation of the body's response to stress. As the amygdala shrinks, the prefrontal cortex – associated with higher order brain functions such as awareness, concentration and decision-making become thicker.[33]

Eureka! It's possible to physically rewire our network of neurons and recover contentment from the stress of overthinking as we redirect our personal energy away from balancing our fears to empowering the fullness of our being. The above study confirms that our efforts contribute to physical changes.

Intentional self-harmonization and mindfulness energize the path to Soul Chatter fluency, but discovering the most effective methods are personal and unique to each person. The best way to develop our mindfulness toolbox is to dive in.

Here are a few common practices to explore and experience. This is not an exhaustive list but, rather, is designed to start you thinking about which methods appeal to you and might have a positive impact on your life:

- Meditation

- Prayer

- Journaling

- Exercise

- Exploring nature

- Sensory awareness exercises

- Practicing gratitude

- Crafts and Hobbies

- Cooking and Baking

Consider exploring these mindful and present-moment-living methods to see which protocols appeal to you. Begin by engaging in one of the practices on a regular basis for a two-month trial, long enough for it to become a habit. At that time, you can continue using it or, if it's unhelpful, proceed to the next technique on the list. With persistence, you will develop tools and habits that support your Soul Chatter lifestyle.

Harmonize Your Inner Children
Being Fully Present and Allowing Your Inner Children to Have a Voice

Our authentic self brings along with it the imperfections of being human. We can be our best while also acknowledging the truth of the worst we can be. When we are honest with ourselves and consider all our parts (including our frayed edges), we can quit spending all our energy manicuring a good veneer and, instead, get real about who we are and why we do the things we do.

As we get comfortable in our own skin, we begin to accept our quirks and appreciate what makes us unique. Taking time to contemplate the parts of us we aren't proud of can bring great insight. Consider the maturing of all our parts. It might be helpful to remember that you entered this world naked and screaming—look how far you've come!

Intentionally allowing our inner children to have a voice in our present and future plans looks a lot like taking a deep breath, slowing down, and considering the end-game of our conflicting desires. During this process of self-acceptance and balancing our ambitions, we get a better glimpse of our holistic self and work to authentically decipher the passions of our heart.

A good way to visualize the harmonizing of our parts is to imagine our inner children out on a road trip, with our being self at the wheel. One of our inner children might want to plan the trip while another wants to be sure everyone is buckled up and supplied with fun snacks. Maybe another inner child is bored and complaining.

Consider that all your inner children's desires are valid, as each of them has much to say about your life journey and the directions you should travel. They are all correct as they see it. But only your being self sees the complete picture. It can recognize the intentions and perspectives of all sides.

Self-harmonization is the process of having your inner children band together for a family meeting, listening to and respecting each other's opinions. The result is the greatest road trip ever—free from chaos, consternation, and passive-aggressive barbs. Soul Chatter fluency energizes the inner connection and accesses the maturity to rise above the inner conflicts and arrive at the best decisions for your journey while simultaneously practicing grace and self-care.

Grace of Self-Acceptance
The Ultimate Act of Self-Care

As our journey to self-harmonization evolves, we become more content with being. Some of the rough edges of our holistic self smooth out in the form of maturity and acceptance. We can master our gifts and chuckle at our flaws as we stop trying to fix who we are and employ the discipline to modify our unproductive behaviors.

We will always experience occasional pangs of emotional pain. We've had a lifetime of weathering storms and experiencing difficult things that chill our soul. That's okay—we can weather the occasional emotional storm. We must not allow self-judgment, guilt, or shame to derail us. Those are emotional states from the past, and we are moving forward. Let's give ourselves fierce grace, just as we would for anyone we love dearly.

Take this moment to celebrate your victory! You have overcome challenges in this life and gained the maturity and wisdom to use your gifts to contribute to a better world for those you love and those who come after you. Commit to the self-care and discipline necessary to live passionately.

Have the courage to embrace the vulnerability necessary to fully connect with yourself and others so that you might love well. It may be helpful to mentally retrace the steps you have traversed during your Soul Chatter journey.

Soul Care: Steps 1-3—You began this journey by choosing to pursue emotional healing and transparency while identifying, examining, and caring for your emotional wound.

Soul Song: Steps 4 & 5—As you experienced emotional healing, you came face-to-face with your worth and fully embraced your value. You could no longer let others assign you roles or write your story, so you claimed your voice and asserted your power. You are forever changed. Your internalized worth can never be taken away from you. No one can diminish your authentic self without your consent—you now control the narrative and have access to the tools to recover when tipped.

Soul Soaring: Steps 6 & 7—As you quieted the outside world, you became aware of your Soul Chatter and the uniqueness of your inner children, including their need to be respected and heard. That awareness unfolds the process of self-harmonization (Step 6). Being fully yourself requires an unmasking while you become comfortable in your own skin.

You now have the option to access the contentment and profound joy of authentic living and may choose to follow your passion to your purpose. This experience will cultivate in you an overwhelming sense of gratitude and a desire to give back.

The important part of fully living your life is that you have the autonomy to make choices. There are no wrong answers. Recognizing that you have the power to live your life however you choose is the freedom of Soul Soaring. Life is short and we have much to do. I hope to meet you again in the clouds.

Chapter Eleven Notes

CHAPTER TWELVE

Step 7: Gratitude and Giving Back

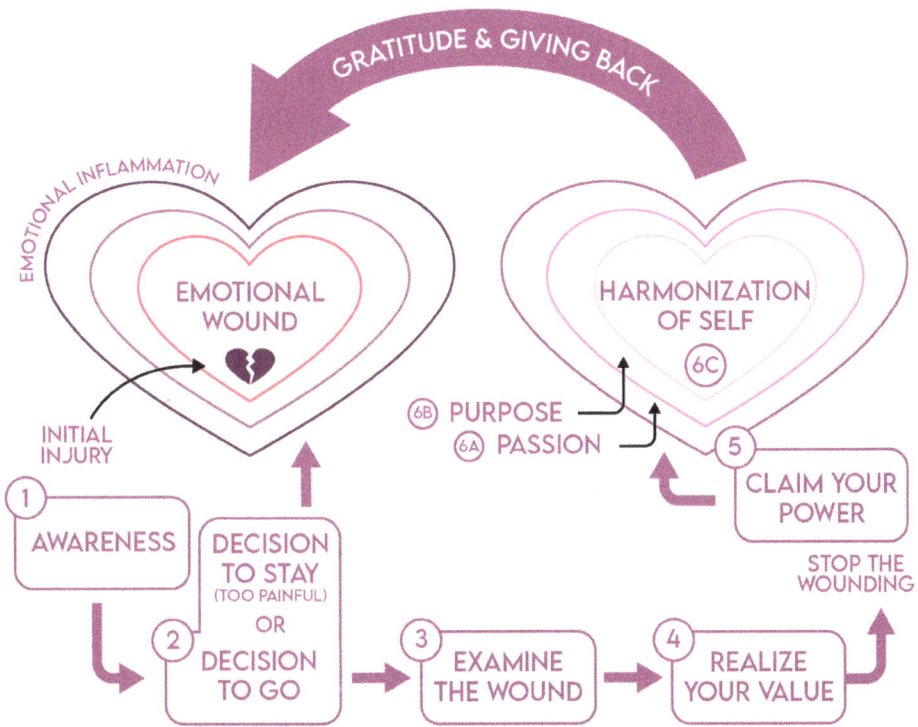

Corbett Model of Emotional Healing & Self-Integration™

> Well and what happened then?
> Well in Whoville they say,
> the Grinch's small heart grew three sizes that day! [34]
> **—Dr. Theodor Seuss Geisel**

A Habit of Gratitude

The final step on our journey to self-harmonization is *gratitude and giving back* (Step 7). This step comes naturally after the others have been fulfilled. When our healing is complete and the urgency to address our own wound fades, we look outward. We can now use our energy and resources to energize our passions and support another wounded soul.

We might visualize emotional healing like an onion. When the time is right, another layer of our wounded self may need peeling. But this time we are ready. We know the process and no longer need to be stuck there.

As we reflect on our Soul Chatter journey and the wisdom received from the process, we are thankful to experience the fullness of life as our emotional wounds scar over. Gratitude is a decision and, over time, becomes a habit. It leads to a sharing of our gifts, and in that process, we get the privilege of supporting fellow soul-journers.

The Grace to Accept Your Being as You Are

Now the big reveal—that *Wizard of Oz* moment when the curtain is drawn open and we see what has been in front of us all this time. Like Dorothy, we have always had the power to go back to our Kansas. We just needed to recognize the distractions and trust the wisdom of our Soul Chatter.

As you give yourself permission to delight in who you are, you can breathe easy and bask in confident contentment. Life will unfold as it should, and the resources you need will be available as you need them. Fully living as the person you were created to be is as natural as breathing. You will never be content as anyone other than yourself.

Do you remember that sweet toddler who embodied the soul-soaring freedom to belly flop into the puddle? She instinctively *knew* what most of us spend a lifetime wrestling with: everything we need to live a passionate life of purpose, gratitude, and giving back is already tucked within our being.

Independent of circumstance, you are exactly who you need to be to live a full and productive life, and no one can take that away. You are extraordinarily gifted with the talents and experiences that give you the abilities and insights to make your unique contribution.

From the beginning of human existence until the end of time, only *you* can live the life you were born to live. No other human but you can do this. Your mission is to weave your personal panache into the tapestry of humanity. Without you, a thread will forever be missing.

Love Gains Power When It Is Freely Given

As we complete the steps on our Soul Chatter journey, we gain confidence and learn to trust the process. We can delight in the pursuit of our passions and recognize their importance as energizing fuel for our lives.

Our passion may become a message when it connects to another person's life: A poem may become a hug that invokes change in another human's spirit. A song may sustain someone through a dark night. The art of baking may produce a cake that reminds someone of their special value. All our gifts can become hope for others on their own journeys, and that is the state-of-being joy and power of giving back. Don't judge it, just do it.

By having the courage to fully embody the person we were created to be, we can effect change and offer hope to others. Recognizing this truth affirms and encourages us to have faith in our pursuits and to be confident in the authenticity of our being.

Your Butterfly Moment

It's your time. Spread your spotted wings and follow your passions. Let go of any guilt or shame that blocks your flow. Do not judge your message—your job is simply to create and release. Focus on your mission and enjoy fully living as you.

> "Hope" is the thing with feathers—
> That perches in the soul.[35]
>
> **—Emily Dickinson**

A Life Story
Living Well

This story is yours. It contains starts and stops and grand adventures. I have provided a few questions to spark some flow and get you started. Your next chapter is yours to write.

My Childhood:

As a child, I loved to _____

_____

As a teenager, I was especially good at _____

_____

Looking back, I always enjoyed _____

_____

I considered a passion of mine to be _____

_____

A time I loved well was _____

_____

Vision Statements

When I think back over my life, I have felt most energized when I _____

_____

I am most grateful for _____

_____

An obstacle for me is _____

_____

The antidote to that obstacle is _____

_____

I am most looking forward to _____

_____

Giving Back
Shhh...It's Never Been about You

Emotional healing requires a space of self-reflection and self-contemplation. Truly understanding the complexities of our being demands our full attention, and by its very nature, intense healing can be a time of self-absorption.

Similarly, our Soul Chatter journey to self-harmonization has necessarily been a deep dive into the messiness and tangled threads of life. This has required intense focus and a great deal of our personal energy. Now, as we use that energy to live a Soul Chatter lifestyle, we can commit to:

- Letting go of any shame or blame we still harbor. They are the true enemy of our authentic selves. We are not perfect and deserve the grace we would give a person we love.

- Focusing on the present moment and understanding that our journey has shaped us into the person we are today.

- Experiencing the self-grace to be set free from self-absorption. A big, beautiful world awaits, and we have work to do.

As you complete this last step of your *Emotional Healing and Self-Harmonization* journey, you now have the tools to reside in a place of contented clarity and can victoriously declare your deep dive into personal healing complete.

From this place of gratitude and giving back, you can allow life to unfold and be expectant. You can accept that you will never be perfect, yet be assured that you are a perfect version of you.

Sozo Exercise:
Gratitude

The Rise and Rest of Gratitude

The Habit of Thankfulness

<u>Intention</u>: Our behaviors become habits, and habits become a way of life. The attitude of gratitude begins with the commitment to focus on the positive and acknowledge what we are thankful for in this life.

Action:

Learn the 5, 4, 3, 2, 1 gratitude habit and, for ten consecutive days, practice it as you lie down to bed and as you get up in the morning.

Name **5** things you are grateful for.

Think of **4** things that made you smile or laugh.

Recall **3** recent events that worked out in your favor.

Think of **2** people in your life who have been kind to you or whom you appreciate.

Think of **1** thing you are looking forward to in the near future.

Breathe, smile, and be grateful.

Chapter Twelve Notes

One Last Letter from Virginia

Dear Soul-journer,

This is where I really wish I could hug you. What a journey—you did it!

Our Soul Chatter journey continues for each of us in our respective life stages. Along the way, we can count on awe-inspiring exhilaration, frustration, disappointments, and surprises.

As my own life continues, I will revel in the beautiful moments and pucker during those "bitter pill" occasions. And I will occasionally find myself wondering, "Why didn't someone tell me this would happen?" In an effort to soften those times for others, I've begun a list below.

Helpful Things to Know
Feel free to add your own!

- Your future career may not even exist yet. Keep following your passion, even if you aren't sure where it is leading you.

- Avocados keep incredibly long if kept submerged in water in the fridge. Don't stress about overripe fruit.

- Wholeheartedly love the people currently in your life. Wonderful friendships can be for just a season. And some can be picked up where you last left off.

- There is never a time to "rest on your laurels." If you are a hard worker in the earlier part of your life, plan on working hard in the latter part also.

- Change is certain. Enjoy every moment.

- Know your priorities. You can drop every plate you are spinning, but don't forsake the people you love.

- Don't define success by the world's terms. Doing something that scares you is a success in itself.

- With any act that is true to your authentic self, courageous living begins by taking baby steps.

During my thousands of hours exploring the emotional wounds of others, a few journeys have stood out to me. They all have some things in common. These are people who dare to deeply connect to their Soul Chatter. They trust the process and shed each layer of their protective outer shell to blossom into their potential. They live on their own terms, courageously ignoring judgment and criticism. They understand their value and the urgency that comes with the brevity of life.

Let your connection to your Soul Chatter fluency guide your own baby step into your next adventure. Stay true to who you are by employing your gifts and talents. Your courage will inspire others as you traverse the beauty of a life well lived.

With deep admiration,

Virginia

Desiderata

Max Ehrmann (1927) [36]

Go placidly amid the noise and haste
and remember what peace there may be in silence.
As far as possible, without surrender, be on good terms with all persons.
Speak your truth quietly and clearly; and listen to others,
even to the dull and ignorant; they too have their story.

Avoid loud and aggressive persons, they are vexations to the spirit.
If you compare yourself with others, you may become vain and bitter,
for always there will be greater and lesser persons than yourself.
Enjoy your achievements as well as your plans.

Keep interested in your own career, however humble;
it is a real possession in the changing fortunes of time.
Exercise caution in your business affairs, for the world is full of trickery.
But let this not blind you to what virtue there is;
many persons strive for high ideals,
and everywhere life is full of heroism.

Be yourself. Especially do not feign affection. Neither be cynical about love;
for in the face of all aridity and disenchantment it is as perennial as the grass.
Take kindly the counsel of the years, gracefully surrendering the things of youth.
Nurture strength of spirit to shield you in sudden misfortune.
But do not distress yourself with dark imaginings.
Many fears are born of fatigue and loneliness.

Beyond a wholesome discipline, be gentle with yourself.
You are a child of the universe no less than the trees and the stars;
you have a right to be here. And whether or not it is clear to you,
no doubt the universe is unfolding as it should.

Therefore be at peace with God, whatever you conceive Him to be.
And whatever your labors and aspirations, in the noisy confusion of life,
keep peace with your soul.
With all its sham, drudgery and broken dreams,
it is still a beautiful world. Be cheerful. Strive to be happy

.

Soul Chatter Quick Reference Manual

For a quick refresher (or for the less patient sojourner), here is a guide to help you become fluent in the language of your soul. You will find an overview of the seven-step model and a brief description of the supporting tools.

Emotional Healing & Self-Harmonization Model

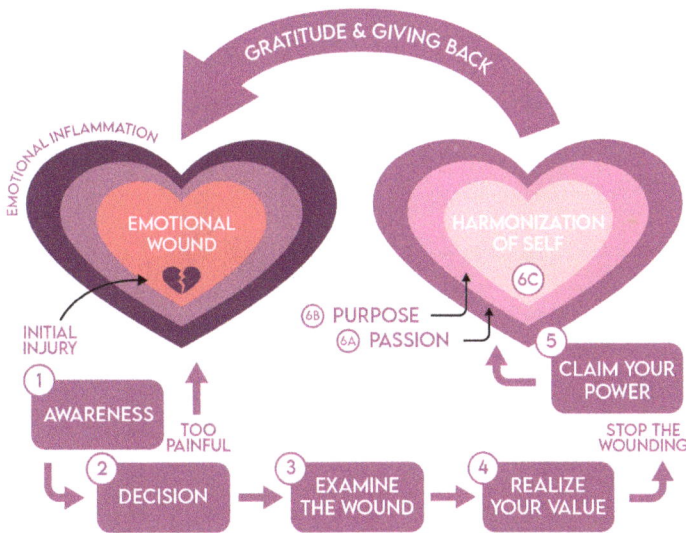

Corbett Model of Emotional Healing & Self-Harmonization™

The Corbett Model of Emotional Healing & Self-Harmonization™ is a seven-step model that will guide you along your journey. Although each step builds on the previous, they are independent and can be addressed as you feel led.

Soul Chatter Sub-Sections

For the purpose of clarity, the seven steps to Soul Chatter fluency are broken into three phases.

Soul Care: Section 1 is an overview of *Steps 1* and *2*, in which we explore emotional wounds and gain understanding of the emotional healing process. Here we learn the importance of caring for our Soul.

Soul Song: Section 2 gives voice to the melody that hums from each of our beings, leading us through *Steps 3, 4*, and *5*. We accept our personal value and the resulting desire to claim our power as we find the voice of empowerment.

Soul Soaring: Section 3 explores the freedom of uncovering our authentic passions and discovering our purpose. This section covers *Steps 6* and *7*, leading us through the final step of self-harmonization. Our journey culminates in a desire to reach beyond our own needs and give back to a hurting world.

Sozo Life Stories

The *Sozo Life Stories* shared in this guidebook are portraits of the healing journeys of some courageous people I have been privileged to know, work with, and admire. Their struggles and insights toward achieving Soul Chatter fluency may prove helpful.

Their stories detail the thorny process of peeling away defenses and the superficial until all that is left is authentic to our beings. Unless otherwise requested, all identifying details have been altered to respect their privacy.

Sozo Healing Exercises
Your Personalized Recipe for Living

To help you immerse yourself into each step, *Sozo Healing Exercises* are designed to help you move beyond words and toward hands-on participation. The art of sensual learning provides an opportunity for nonverbal conceptualization.

It's most helpful to view these activities as positive and fun—a chance to relax, explore, and smile. As you examine your thoughts and connect corresponding feelings, you may experience an associated emotion. It could be silly, pleasant, or even uncomfortable.

Tapping into unexplored emotions can be cathartic and healing, but as with any journey, you may find an unexpected bump or unexplored bend along the way. If you have difficulties processing any of these feelings, I encourage you to consult a professional therapist.

Spirituality

We are holistic beings—mind, body, spirit—and to neglect any of those parts will create a deficit. Your spiritual journey is unique to you; no other human can judge your heart. My personal belief system is Christian, but my sincere desire is to meet you wherever you are on your unique spiritual path.

Soul Chatter is a guide for emotional healing and personal development, and I hope it will provide a spark of encouragement. In my years as a therapist, I have found that healing flourishes when a person feels understood and validated.

Acknowledgments

I would like to express my heartfelt gratitude to the people who have met me in life's dark and sunny spaces, inspired me, and assisted me in the delivery of this decade-long birth of a passion. The truth is, I had to live the story in order to write it, and sometimes other people have to believe in you before you can believe in yourself. *Thank you!*

Thank you, Dianna Frizler, for your whimsical art that created the pizazz empowering the cover of this book! As you have authentically followed your passion, the joy you spread has been contagious.

Thank you, Christina Baker-Kline, for the precious hours you spent encouraging my early attempts at turning inspiration to words.

Thank you, Wenonah Hoye, for your gentle ("let's try this instead") humor, enthusiasm, and support.

Thank you, Baron Batch, for staying true to your authentic self and for your example of selfless generosity.

Thank you, Kelly, for your artistic expression and your ability to see the beauty in the darkness as the ultimate healing workbook unfolds.

Thank you to Joy, Leah, Adam, Mary, Aaron, Caleb, and all of the team at Renown Publishing.

With great respect, I lift my stemless glass in a toast to the strong women who have inspired my journey and have been examples of how diamonds are created. "Cheers!" to:

Mandy—you and my stories are so intertwined. I hardly know where mine stops and yours starts. Thank you for being my "ride or die."

My mother—the original rebel, who wrote her own story. I love you.

Chechee—pioneering adventure burns hot in your DNA. You are strong, inspiringly courageous, and also a gentle, wise soul.

Concon—you will always cut your hair, and there is nothing we can do about it. And we wouldn't want to. Your courage to be authentically unique, fight injustice, and empower creativity is a force that will continue to set the world ablaze.

Nana—you duct-taped and stitched us all together and were my true-north example of strength, grace, and dignity.

Ellie—your courage to leave the farm and pursue the Wild West has inspired generations of adventurers.

Babi—you are the bravest woman I have ever known. You fought for your faith and your family, and you changed the life of everyone who followed.

Ceclia—you were a woman before your time. Your courage and selfless love continue to inspire.

Dyana—we both had our battles to fight, but your stability and humor buoyed my life at a time I was treading water.

Charlotte—I know it was the most chaotic of times, but we figured out who we are and became women who strive to love ourselves and cherish the love we are offered.

Susan—thank you for co-mothering and making up for my chaos while bringing the fun.

Laura—you are both brilliant and wise. Thank you for being my friend and confidant, whom I turn to for discerning counsel.

Linda—there is no one I would rather go through basic training with (even with the plot twists)!

Tammy—I'm so glad our journeys crossed. Your pure heart and pure faith sharpen mine.

Mandy—it's set in stone: "back-door friends are best." You are courageous and strong, and I love you.

Viola—thank you for being my example of faith, joy, and love.

About the Author

Virginia Corbett is a passionate advocate for holistic emotional wellness. Her greatest wish is that we humans would be excellent at loving and supporting each other. She has been blessed to work with dedicated people who do just that.

During her years of providing psychotherapy and integrative-wellness workshops, Virginia developed a 7-step model to help clients achieve the goal of self-harmonization and becoming their best selves.

Virginia is a recovering serial entrepreneur and has been featured in:

- *Forbes Magazine,* "Secrets of Success from Midlife Entrepreneurs"

- Kerry Hannon's book, *You Are Never Too Old to Get Rich*

- *Whirl Magazine,* "Powerful Pittsburgh Women"

- *Money Magazine,* "Second Acts"

About Renown Publishing

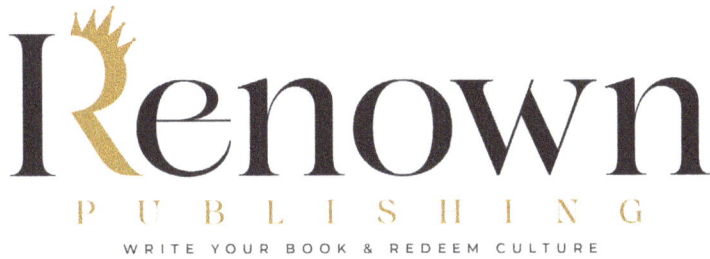

Renown Publishing is the proud publishing imprint of Speak It To Book, an elite team of publishing professionals devoted to helping you shape, write, and share your book. Renown has written, edited, and worked on hundreds of books (including New York Times, Wall Street Journal, and USA Today best-sellers, and the #1 book on all of Amazon).

We believe authentic stories are the torch of change-makers, and our mission is to collaborate with purpose-driven authors to create societal impact and redeem culture.

If you're the founder of a purpose-driven company, visit RenownPublishing.com.

If you're an aspiring author, visit SpeakItToBook.com.

Notes

1. Roedel, John, "Become! Become! Become!" John Roedel (blog). December 10, 2020. https://www.johnroedel.com/post/manage-your-blog-from-your-live-site.

2. *Blue Letter Bible,* "Strong's G4982 – sōzō." https://www.blueletterbible.org/lexicon/g4982/kjv/tr/0-1.

3. Dennis, Patrick. *Auntie Mame: An Irreverent Escapade.* Vanguard Press, 1955.

4. The origin of the Serenity Prayer is frequently disputed, but Reinhold Niebuhr and/or Winnifred Crane Wygal are generally credited. Circa 1932.

5. Stewig, John Warren. "Nonverbal Communication: "I See What You Say."" *Language Arts* 56, no. 2 (1979): p. 150–55. https://www.jstor.org/stable/41404774.

6. Baum, Frank L. *The Wizard of Oz.* George M. Hill Company, 1900.

7. Kondo, Marie. *The Life-Changing Magic of Tidying Up: The Japanese Art of Decluttering and Organizing.* New York: Ten Speed Press, 2014.

8. Dr. Aaron T. Beck founded Cognitive Behavioral Therapy in the 1960s. For more information, see: Chand, Suma P., Daniel P. Kuckel, and Martin R. Huecker. "Cognitive Behavior Therapy." *StatPearls* (March 2023). StatPearls Publishing, 2023. https://www.ncbi.nlm.nih.gov/books/NBK470241/#.

9. Tzu, Sun. *The Art of War: The Ancient Classic.* Capstone Publishing, 2010.

10. Davison, Peter, "Robert Frost: The Cost of Friendship" *The Washington Post.* July 5, 1981. https://www.washingtonpost.com/archive/entertainment/books/1981/07/05/robert-frost-the-cost-of-friendship/487a848b-8295-4226-a25a-11604ab53310/.

11. Wright, Abdul. "Unapologetically Equitable in Action." In *10 Perspective on Equity in Education,* edited by Jimmy Casas, Onica L. Mayers, and Jeffrey Zoul. Routledge, 2021.

12. C, Sreechinth. *Musings of Carl Jung.* UB Tech, 2018.

13. Swartz, Richard C. *Internal Family Systems Therapy.* The Guildford Press, 2019.

Holmes, Tom. *Parts Work: An Illustrated Guide to You Inner Life.* Winged Heart Press, 2007.

14. van der Kolk, Bessel A. *The Body Keeps the Score.* Penguin, 2014.

15. Shakespeare. Julius Caesar. Act 2, Scene 2. Lines 1008–09. https://www.opensourceshakespeare.org/views/plays/play_view.php?WorkID=juliuscaesar&Act=2&Scene=2&Scope=scene.

16. Dickenson, Emily. "A wounded deer leaps highest." In *Poems.* 1891.

17. Stromberg, Robert, dir. *Maleficent.* Walt Disney Studios, 2014.

18. Warren, Rick. *A Purpose Driven Life.* Zondervan, 2002.

19. West, Maxine. "Peoplemaking: Esteem or Shame?" In *Virginia Satir: Foundational Ideas,* edited by Barbara Jo Brothers. Routledge, 1991.

20. Bowen, Murray. Quoted in Dara Gasior. "Differentiation of Self." *Family Therapy Techniques: Working with Challenging Families.* High Focus Centers. https://www.monmouth.edu/graduate/documents/family-therapy-working-with-challenging-family-dynamics-in-effective-manner.pdf.

21. Rand, Ayn. *The Fountainhead.* Bobbs Merill, 1943.

22. Wilde, Oscar. "The Soul of the Man Under Socialism." *Fortnightly Review.* February 1891, p. 292.

23. Cummings, E. E. "A Poet's Advice to Students." *Ottawa Hills Spectator.* October 26, 1955. Quoted in *E. E. Cummings: A Miscellany Revised.* October House, 1965.

24. Roth, Eric, screenwriter. *The Curious Case of Benjamin Button.* Directed by David Fincher. Paramount, 2008.

25. Frankl, Viktor E. *Man's Search for Meaning.* Beacon Press, 1959.

26. Frankl, Viktor E. In Patricia Starck, "Logotherapy: A Conversation with Viktor Frankl, MD, PhD." UT School of Nursing. June 21, 1985. YouTube video. https://www.youtube.com/watch?v=yNNokZcKX0Y.

27. Ehrmann, Max. "Desiderata." In *The Poems of Max Ehrmann.* B. Humphries, 1948.

28. Angelou, Maya. *Rainbow in the Cloud: The Wisdom and Spirit of Maya Angelou.* Random House Publishing, 2014.

29. Acuff, Jon. *Soundtracks: The Surprising Solution to Overthinking.* Baker Books, 2021.

30. Frost, Robert. *Poetry for Young People.* Sterling, 1994.

31. Goldthwait, Bobcat, dir. *World's Greatest Dad.* Magnolia Pictures, 2009.

32. Smith, Andrew Fox, dir. *A Harmonious Life.* 2020. https://www.youtube.com/watch?v=w8xEGEtg97E.

33. Taren, Adrienne A., J. David Creswell, and Peter J. Gianaros. "Dispositional Mindfulness Co-varies with Smaller Amygdala and Caudate Volumes in Community Adults." *Plos One* (2013). https://doi.org/10.1371/journal.pone.0064574.

34. Seuss, Dr. *How the Grinch Stole Christmas!* Random House Publishing, 1957.

35. Dickenson, Emily. "'Hope' is the thing with feathers." In *Poems*. 1891.

36. Ehrmann, *Desiderata*.